C000000966

Author: Yussuf Hamad BSc. Eng, MBA Finance

THIS BOOK BELONGS TO:	
SCHOOL	
CLASS	
YEAR	

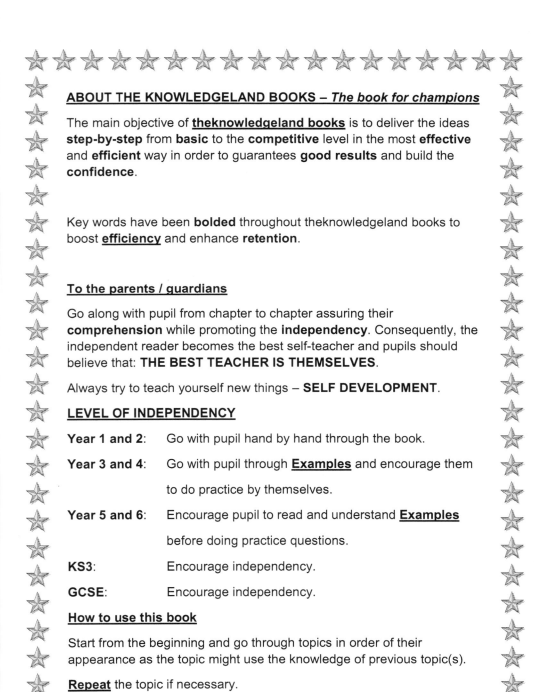

ABOUT THE KNOWLEDGELAND BOOKS – *The book for champions*

The main objective of **theknowledgeland books** is to deliver the ideas **step-by-step** from **basic** to the **competitive** level in the most **effective** and **efficient** way in order to guarantees **good results** and build the **confidence**.

Key words have been **bolded** throughout theknowledgeland books to boost **efficiency** and enhance **retention**.

To the parents / guardians

Go along with pupil from chapter to chapter assuring their **comprehension** while promoting the **independency**. Consequently, the independent reader becomes the best self-teacher and pupils should believe that: **THE BEST TEACHER IS THEMSELVES**.

Always try to teach yourself new things – **SELF DEVELOPMENT**.

LEVEL OF INDEPENDENCY

Year 1 and 2:   Go with pupil hand by hand through the book.

Year 3 and 4:   Go with pupil through **Examples** and encourage them to do practice by themselves.

Year 5 and 6:   Encourage pupil to read and understand **Examples** before doing practice questions.

KS3:   Encourage independency.

GCSE: Encourage independency.

How to use this book

Start from the beginning and go through topics in order of their appearance as the topic might use the knowledge of previous topic(s).

Repeat the topic if necessary.

THEKNOWLEDGELAND BOOKS – BOOKS FOR CHAMPS
www.theknowledgeland.co.uk

CODE	BOOK NAME	ISBN NUMBER
01	MATH YEAR 1 (AGE 5 - 6)	B08F9W214L
02	MATH YEAR 2 (AGE 6 - 7)	B08F6Y3VYR
03	MATH KS1 (AGE 5 - 7)	B08F6JZC46
04	MATH YEAR 3 (AGE 7 - 8)	B08F6JZC52
05	MATH YEAR 4 (AGE 8 - 9)	B08F6QNWHJ
06	MATH YEAR 5 (AGE 9 - 10)	B08F6RCCLN
07	MATH YEAR 6 (AGE 10 - 11)	B08F7VFTST
08	MATH KS2 (AGE 7 - 11)	B08F6MVKYR
09	MATH KS3 (AGE 11 - 14)	B08F65SBM7
10	MATH GCSE (AGE 14 - 16)	B08F6MVL8K
11	ENGLISH YEAR 1 (AGE 5 - 6)	B08FP4MN8S
12	ENGLISH YEAR 2 (AGE 6 - 7)	B08FBMFBDD
13	ENGLISH KS1 (AGE 5 - 7)	B08F7VFTST
14	ENGLISH YEAR 3 (AGE 7 - 8)	B08FKS7Y73
15	ENGLISH YEAR 4 (AGE 8 - 9)	B08F7YWTX9
16	ENGLISH YEAR 5 (AGE 9 - 10)	B08F7QL781
17	ENGLISH YEAR 6 (AGE 10 - 11)	B08F7GP4NS
18	ENGLISH KS2 (AGE 7 - 11)	B08FKQNL1R
19	ENGLISH KS3 (AGE 11 - 14)	
20	ENGLISH GCSE (AGE 14 - 16)	

THE CONTENTS

1. NUMBERS

- **NUMBER LINE**
- **SCALE READING**
- **TREND**

NUMBER LINE

- Uses the number line to add and subtract the numbers.
- When **adding**, move **step to the right**.
- When **subtracting**, move **step to the left**.

Example:

Work out: $4 - 7 =$ [start at 4 and move 7 steps to the left]

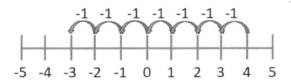

$$4 - 7 = -3$$

SCALE READING

Read the same as number line.

Example: The number in speedometer below

are shown in miles per hour (MPH).

Read the speedometer below.

Answer

54 MPH

TRENDS

Trends are series of numbers that follow **particular rules**.

Each number is called a **term.**

Example:

Trend: 30, 27, 24, 21, ..   →**Rule: -3**

Trend: 3, 9, 27, 81, ...   →**Rule: x3**

Given the rule: **x2, then -1**.

Write down the next three terms of the series: 2,____,____,_____.

Answer

2nd term $(2 \times 2) - 1 = 3$

3rd term $(3 \times 2) - 1 = 5$

4th term $(5 \times 2) - 1 = 9$

So the series is 2, 3, 5, 9

Practice 1

(1)With the aid of the number line work out the following:

(a)$4 - 6 =$ (b)$-10 + 5 =$ (c)$1 - 8 =$ (d)$-8 + 9 =$

(2) Work out the following:

(a) $15 - 25 =$ (b) $75 - 100 =$ (c)$10 - 20 =$

(2)Read the following scales:

(a)

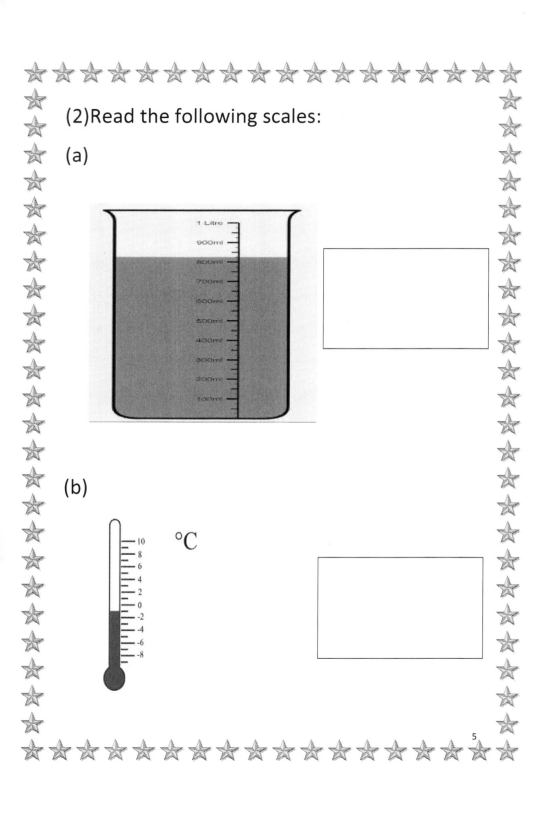

(b)

°C

(3)State the rule and complete the missing numbers in the following trends (series):

a) 1, 6, 11, 16, _____, _____, _____ .

   Rule:.......................

b) 20, 17, 14, _____, _____, _____ .

   Rule:.......................

c) 2, 8, 32, _____, _____, _____ .

   Rule:.......................

(4)Given the rules, complete the following series:

a) Rule: x3, -1

   1, 2, _____, _____, _____ .

b) Rule: -1, x3

   2, 3, _____, _____, _____ .

2. NUMBER OPERATIONS

ADDITIONS AND SUBTRACTIONS

- When adding or subtracting, first, align the numbers <u>from the right</u> the side.

Example

➤ 438 + 69 =

$$4^1 \quad 3^1 \quad 8$$

$$+ \quad \underline{\quad 6 \quad 9}\text{(align from the right side)}$$

$$\underline{5 \quad 0 \quad 7} \textbf{ Answer}$$

So 438 + 69 = 507

➤ 526 – 78 =

$$5 \quad 2 \quad 6$$

$$- \quad \underline{\quad 7 \quad 8}$$

$$\underline{4 \quad 4 \quad 8} \textbf{ Answer}$$

Mental math

Knowing that: 246 − 100 = 146

You can work out mentally 246 - 98

246 − 98 = [246 − 100 + 2] = 148

Practice 2(calculator is <u>NOT</u> allowed)

   (1) 6479 + 179 =

   (2) 9423 − 68 =

   (3) Work out in your head:

      (a)465 − 97 =

      (b)615 + 95 =

      (c)562 − 102 =

   (4) <u>Fill in</u> the missing numbers

	7	2	1	?	9
+		5	6	3	?
?	7	8	1	1

MULTIPLICATIONS AND DIVISIONS

i. MULTIPLICATIONS

- Multiplication is very important in mastering math.

12 X 12 TIMETABLE										
X	2	3	4	5	6	7	8	9	10	11	12
2	4	6	8	10	12	14	16	18	20	22	24
3	6	9	12	15	18	21	24	27	30	33	36
4	8	12	16	20	24	28	32	36	40	44	48
5	10	15	20	25	30	35	40	45	50	55	60
6	12	18	24	30	36	42	48	54	60	66	72
7	14	21	28	35	42	49	56	63	70	77	84
8	16	24	32	40	48	56	64	72	80	88	96
9	18	27	36	45	54	63	72	81	90	99	108
10	20	30	40	50	60	70	80	90	100	110	120
11	22	33	44	55	66	77	88	99	110	121	132
12	24	36	48	60	72	84	96	108	120	132	144

Practice 3

Fill in the missing numbers						
X	9	7	6	4	8	3
2	18					
7		49				
3			18			
8				32		
11					88	
4						12
6					48	
5				20		
12			72			
9		63				
10	90					

Mental math

When multiplying, ignore 'end-zeros' then replace them in the answer

Example

30 x 500= (3 x 5)000 =15000

If someone asked you to touch your right ear you can use your left hand, pass it over your head and touch your right ear! Right? BUT it is quicker to touch it with your right hand. So,

When doing math, use the method which is quicker for you so you can **save time.**

Multiplying 20x3 is easier than 15x4

Example: work out 5 x 3 x 4

5 x 3 x 4 = 5 x 4 x 3 [no need to follow the order] = 20 x 3 = 60

Practice 4 (Mental math)

(1) 7000 x 30 =

(2) 42 x 3 =

(3) 4200 x 30 =

(4) 5 x 9 x 2 =

LONG MULTIPLICATION

Multiply 5379 x 26

5379 x 26 = (multiply each number by 2 then

Multiply each by 6 and then add them)

```
        5   3   7   9
    x           2   6

    1   0   7   5   8        (5379 x 2)

+       3   2   2   7   4    (5379 x 6)

    1   3   9   8   5   4  Answer
```

So 5379 x 26 = 139854

ii. **DIVISIONS**

[cancelation method]

$$\frac{4722^{1574}}{3^1} \left[\frac{how\ many\ 3s\ are\ in\ 4722\ (1574)}{how\ many\ 3s\ are\ in\ 3\ (1)}\right] = 1574$$

LONG DIVISION

Repeat the process: (**÷, x, -, drop**) until there is no more number to divide.

Example: Work out   888 ÷ 37 =

(Repeat (**÷, x - , drop**) three times)

```
      0   2   4
  37)8   8   8    (÷)[8÷37=0]
-   0             (x)[0x37=0]
    8   8         (-)[8-0=8] (drop 8)(÷)[88÷37=2]
-   7   4         (x)[2x37=74]
    1   4   8     (-)[88-74=14] (drop 8)(÷)[148÷37]
-   1   4   8     (x)[4x37=148]
    0   0   0     (-)[148-148=0]
```

Practice 5 (Calculator is <u>NOT</u> allowed)

Work out the following:

(1) 14391 ÷ 3 =

(2) 1000 ÷ 8 =

(3) 8051 ÷ 83 =

(4) 725 ÷ 29 =

PROBLEM SOLVING

When solving problem no one tells you whether you need to multiply or divide the numbers to get to answer. <u>YOU NEED TO THINK</u> what to do to get to the answer.

Example: you need to

+ to get **total (sum)**

− to get **difference**

x if there is **repetition**

÷ if there is **sharing**

Total (+) and difference (-)

The <u>maximum weight</u> that lift can carry is <u>150kg</u>. Sean weighs <u>55kg</u> carrying a bag of <u>5kg</u>. Jamal weighs <u>50kg</u> carrying a bag weighs <u>3kg</u>. Jaden weighs <u>25kg</u>.

(a) Can they all go into the lift with their bags in one go? Illustrate.

(b) How much more weight that they can carry?

Answer

(a) Their total weight is 55 + 5 + 50 + 3 + 25 = 133kg. So <u>yes</u> they can <u>because</u> their total weight (133kg) is less than (150kg) maximum weight that the lift can carry.

(b) They can carry 150 − 133 = 17kg more.

Repetition (x) and sharing (÷)

➢ Sumaiyah is having a birthday party and she has invited <u>30 friends</u>. She wants everyone to have <u>at least one cup cake</u>. Cup cake is sold in the <u>pack of 4</u>. <u>How many packs</u> she should buy?

Answer

She should buy $\frac{30}{4} = 7.5(round\ up)$= 8 packs.

(8 x 4 cup cakes = 32 cup cakes (two cakes extra))

➤   Sumaiyah estimated that <u>each</u> of her friends will drink <u>1.5 litres</u> of juice at the party. How many <u>litres of juice</u> she should prepare?

<u>Answer</u>

1.5 x 30 = 45 litres of juice.

<u>Practice 6</u>

(1) Veronica bought a sandwich cost £1.50, a pack of crisp cost 75p and a bottle of drink cost £1.20. She paid £5 note. How much change she got back?

(2) At a particular time the temperature at Warsaw was 21°c and the temperature in London was 32°c. How many more degrees in London than in Warsaw?

(3) Lucy is having a birthday party and she has invited 40 friends. She wants each friend to have one cup cake. Cup cakes are sold in a pack of 4 each pack costs 95p. How much would Lucy spend for cup cakes?

(4) A kilogram of tomatoes costs £2 and a kilogram of potatoes costs £1.6. Emmanuel buys $1\frac{1}{2}$ kilogram of tomatoes and $\frac{3}{4}$ kilogram of potatoes. How much change does he get from £5?

(5) The knowledgeland strawberry farm

The knowledgeland strawberry farm has 700 rows of strawberry plants each row have 500 plants.

(a) How many strawberry plants are in the farm?

(b) Each plant produces 150g of strawberry. How many grams of strawberry does the farm produce?

(6) Each 100g of duck takes 5 minutes to cook.
How long does it take for 3.5kg duck to cook?

3. TYPES OF NUMBERS

- FACTORS AND MULTIPLES
- EVEN, ODD AND PRIME NUMBERS
- PRIME FACTORS
- SQUARE AND CUBE NUMBERS

FACTORS AND MULTIPLES

FACTORS

A factor is a number that divides into another number exactly without remainder.

Example:

Factors of 20 are: 1, 2, 4, 5, 10 and 20

Factors of 30 are: 1, 2, 3, 5, 6, 10, 15 and 30

The **common factors** of 20 and 30 are: 1, 2, 5 and 10.

The **Highest Common Factor (HCF)** of 20 and 30 is 10.

Practice 9

1) (a) Find the factors of 12 and 18.

   (b) Find their common factors.

   (c) What is the HCF of 12 and 18?

2) Find the HCF of 12 and 24.

MULTIPLES

Multiples are the **products** of the number.

Eg. Multiples of 2 are: 2, 4, 6, 8, 10, 12...

   Multiples of 3 are: 3, 6, 9, 12, 15, 18...

The **common multiples** of 2 and 3 are: 6, 12..

The **Lowest Common Multiple (LCM)** is 6

Practice 10

1) (a) Find the multiples of 3 and 4 which are below 25.

   (b) What are the common multiples?

   (c) What is the Lowest Common Multiple?

2) Find the LCM of 4 and 5.

EVEN, ODD AND PRIME NUMBERS

Even numbers are numbers that can be divided by 2. They end up with 0,2,4,6 and 8.

Eg. 248

Odd numbers are numbers that cannot be divided by 2. They end up with 1,3,5,7 and 9.

Eg. 261.

Prime numbers are numbers which cannot be divided by any number (except by itself and by 1).Eg. 1, 3, 5, 7, ~~9~~, 11, 13, ~~15~~, 17, 19, ~~21~~...

Prime factors are factors that are prime. Eg. The prime factors of 15 are 5 and 3.(because 5x3=15 and 5 and 3 are prime numbers.

Any number can be expressed as a product of prime numbers.

Eg: 100= 2 x 2 x 5 x 5

Because 2 and 5 are prime numbers

SQUARES AND CUBES NUMBERS

Square numbers are: 1, 4, 9, 16, 25, 36, 49..

Cube numbers are: 1, 8, 27, 64...:

Practice 11

(1) $7^2 + 10 =$

(2) $3^3 - 7 =$

(3) Consider the number 1 to 15 as listed below:

1, 2, 3, 4, 5, 6, 7, 8, 9, 10, 11, 12, 13,14 and 15

Place the numbers in the correct card. (You can use a number more than once).

Factors of 30	Multiples of 3	Prime numbers

(4) Express the following numbers as the product of prime numbers.

(a) 200

(b) 120

(c) 360

4. FRACTONS, DECIMAL AND PERCENTAGES

FRACTIONS

One eighth ($\frac{1}{8}$) of my pizza is missing!!!

Fraction is the number in the form of

$$\frac{A \rightarrow (NUMERATOR)}{B \rightarrow (DENOMINATOR)}$$

If A < B the fraction is **Proper fraction.**

Eg. $\frac{2}{3}$ (Two third)

If A > B it is **improper fraction.** Eg. $\frac{3}{2}$

Improper fraction can be changed into **mixed fraction** (whole number + proper fraction). Eg: $1\frac{1}{2}$

CHANGING IMPROPER FRACTION INTO MIXED FRACTION

Change $\frac{11}{4}$ into mixed fraction.

[Ask yourself "how many 4's are in 11? = 2 (whole number), remainder = 3.

→ So $\frac{11}{4}$ = $2\frac{3}{4}$]

To change back into improper fraction:

$$\frac{2 \times 4 + 3}{4} = \frac{11}{4}$$

Q) Change $\frac{10}{3}$ into mixed fraction.

Then change it back to improper fraction.

A) How many 3's are in ten? 3 remain 1

So, $\frac{10}{3} = 3\frac{1}{3}$

$$3\frac{1}{3} = \frac{3 \times 3 + 1}{3} = \frac{10}{3}$$

Practice 12

(1) Change $\frac{20}{3}$ into mixed fraction

(2) Change $2\frac{2}{3}$ into improper fraction

What fraction is the shaded area?

 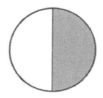 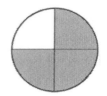

- **The sum of all fraction = 1.**

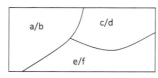

$$\frac{a}{b} + \frac{c}{d} + \frac{e}{f} = 1$$

Example:

Write down the missing fraction so that the total fractions make one thing. $\frac{1}{5} + \frac{3}{10} + \; ? = 1$

27

Answer

$\dfrac{1}{5} + \dfrac{3}{10} + ? = 1$ (make denominator the same)

$\rightarrow \dfrac{2}{10} + \dfrac{3}{10} + ? = 1$

$\rightarrow \dfrac{5}{10} + ? = 1$

$\rightarrow ? = 1 - \dfrac{5}{10} = \dfrac{1}{2}$ $\qquad \left[\dfrac{10}{10} - \dfrac{5}{10} = \dfrac{5}{10} = \dfrac{1}{2} \right]$

Practice 13

(1) What fraction is the shaded area?

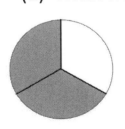

(2) Draw any shape and shade the fractions:

(a) $\dfrac{2}{5}$ (b) $\dfrac{1}{3}$ (c) $\dfrac{5}{6}$

(3) What is the value of the missing fraction?

Divide both numerator and denominator by the same number

Simplify the following fractions:

(a)$\frac{4}{24}$

$$\frac{4}{24} = [\frac{4 \div 4}{24 \div 4}] = \frac{1}{6}$$

(b) $\frac{18}{27}$

$$\frac{18}{27} = [\frac{18 \div 9}{27 \div 9}] = \frac{2}{3}$$

Practice 14

<u>Simplify</u> the following fractions:

1) $\dfrac{4}{28} =$

2) $\dfrac{5}{45} =$

3) $\dfrac{3}{27} =$

4) $\dfrac{12}{18} =$

5) $\dfrac{15}{20} =$

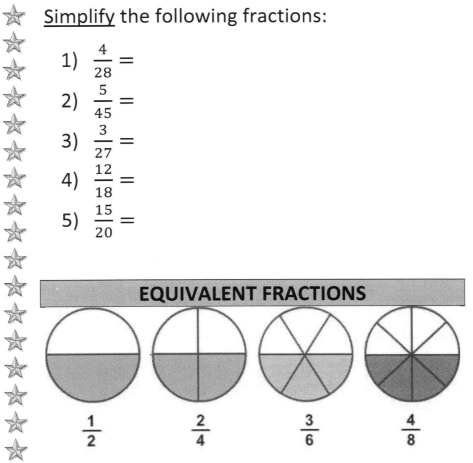

EQUIVALENT FRACTIONS

$\dfrac{1}{2}$ $\dfrac{2}{4}$ $\dfrac{3}{6}$ $\dfrac{4}{8}$

Equivalent fractions are the fractions which have the **same value in their simplest form.**

<u>**Example:**</u> $\dfrac{1}{2} = \dfrac{2}{4} = \dfrac{3}{6} = \dfrac{4}{8}$

30

For a given fraction, you can **multiply** or **divide** both **top and bottom** number by the **same number** <u>without changing the value.</u>

Example

➤ $\frac{6}{9} = [\frac{6 \times 2}{9 \times 2}] = \frac{12}{18}$

➤ $\frac{6}{8} = [\frac{6 \div 2}{8 \div 2}] = \frac{3}{4}$

Complete the missing numbers

➤ $\frac{4}{6} = \frac{2}{} = \frac{}{12}$

$\frac{4}{6} = \frac{4 \div 2}{6 \div 2} = \frac{2}{3} \,,\, \frac{4}{6} = \frac{4 \times 2}{6 \times 2} = \frac{8}{12}$

Practice 15

(1) Complete the missing numbers

$$\frac{8}{10} = \frac{}{5} = \frac{16}{}$$

(2) Which of the following fractions is equivalent to $\frac{3}{9}$?

$$\frac{3}{10}, \quad \frac{6}{9}, \quad \frac{6}{18},$$

(3) Which of the following fractions is <u>NOT</u> equivalent to $\frac{4}{10}$?

$$\frac{2}{5}, \quad \frac{4}{20}, \quad \frac{8}{20}$$

ADDITION AND SUBTRACTION OF FRACTIONS
A) FRACTIONS WITH THE **SAME DENOMINATORS**

Add or take away numerators, but denominators remain the same.

Example

Work out the following then simplify:

a) $\frac{5}{8} + \frac{1}{8}$

$$\frac{5}{8} + \frac{1}{8} = \frac{5+1}{8} = \frac{6}{8} = [\frac{6\div2}{8\div2}] = \frac{3}{4}$$

$b) \frac{5}{6} - \frac{2}{6}$

$$\frac{5}{6} - \frac{2}{6} = \frac{5-2}{6} = \frac{3}{6} = \left[\frac{3 \div 3}{6 \div 3}\right] = \frac{1}{2}$$

B) FRACTIONS WITH **DIFFERENT DENOMINATORS**

First: Make denominator the same.

Example:

Work out the following:

a) $\frac{1}{4} + \frac{1}{2}$

$$\frac{1}{4} + \frac{1}{2} = \left[\frac{1}{4} + \frac{1 x 2}{2 x 2}\right] = \frac{1}{4} + \frac{2}{4} = \frac{3}{4}$$

b) $\frac{1}{3} + \frac{2}{5}$

$$\frac{1}{3} + \frac{2}{5} = \left[\frac{1 x 5}{3 x 5} + \frac{2 x 3}{5 x 3}\right] = \frac{5}{15} + \frac{6}{15} = \frac{11}{15}$$

33

Practice 16

Work out the following fractions and give the answer in its <u>simplest form</u>.

(1) $\frac{1}{9} + \frac{5}{9} =$

(2) $\frac{8}{15} + \frac{4}{15} =$

(3) $\frac{1}{2} + \frac{1}{3} =$

(4) $\frac{4}{5} - \frac{3}{4} =$

(5) $\frac{1}{3} - \frac{1}{4} =$

(6) $1 - \frac{2}{3} =$

MIXED FRACTIONS

<u>Example</u> work out the following:

$$1\frac{1}{5} + 2\frac{3}{5} =$$

$$1\frac{1}{5} + 2\frac{3}{5} = \frac{6}{5} + \frac{13}{5} = \frac{19}{5} = 3\frac{4}{5}$$

Or (add up whole numbers and fractions separately)

$$1\frac{1}{5} + 2\frac{3}{5} = (1+2)\frac{1}{5} + \frac{3}{5} = 3\frac{4}{5}$$

MULTIPLICATION AND DIVISION OF FRACTIONS

When multiplying; cancel numerator with denominator.

<u>Example</u>

Work out the following:

➢ (a) $\frac{3}{4}$ x $\frac{2}{6}$ =

$$\frac{3^1}{4^2} \; x \; \frac{2^1}{6^2} = \frac{1x1}{2x2} = \frac{1}{4}$$

➢ $\frac{3}{4}$ x 10 =

$$\frac{3}{4^2} \; x \; \cancel{10}^5 = \frac{15}{2} = 7\frac{1}{2}$$

➢ $2\frac{2}{3}$ x $\frac{3}{5}$ =

$$2\frac{2}{3} \; x \; \frac{3}{4} = \frac{8}{3^1} \; x \; \frac{3^1}{5} = \frac{8}{5} = 1\frac{3}{5}$$

Practice 17

Work out the following:

(1) $\dfrac{13}{6} - \dfrac{4}{6} =$

(2) $\dfrac{2}{3} + \dfrac{3}{4} =$

(3) $1 + \dfrac{1}{100} =$

(4) $1\dfrac{1}{4} + 2\dfrac{3}{5} =$

(5) $\dfrac{12}{5} \, x \, \dfrac{10}{3} =$

(6) $\dfrac{2}{7} x \, 28 =$

(7) $1\dfrac{1}{3} \, x \, \dfrac{9}{8} =$

(8) $2\dfrac{3}{4} \div 2\dfrac{3}{4} =$

(9) $2\dfrac{1}{3} \div \dfrac{21}{9} =$

(10) $1 - \dfrac{2}{100} =$

DECIMALS

THE FACTS ABOUT DECIMAL POINTS

- Every number has (omitted) decimal point at the end.

Example: 7 = 7.

- The "end zero" after decimal point does not change the value of the number.

Example: 7 = 7.0 or 7 = 7.000   2.5 = 2.50

- Zero before the number does not change the value.

Example: 7 = 07 or 7 = 007

- Zero before the decimal point does not change the value.

Example: .25 = 0.25 or 002.5 = 0.25

However, zero between decimal point and the number **does** change the value.

Example: 0.1 > 0.01

Practice 14

(1)

State whether the statement is True or False			
4.50	=	4.5	
0.05	=	0.5	

0.7	=	7	
007	=	7	
4	=	4.00	

(2)

Pace <, > or = to make the statement correct		
2		2.0
3.9		3.10
4.01		4.10
0.20		0.19
10		010
07		70
0.1		0.20
0.1		0.01

ADITION AND SUBTRACTION OF DECIMALS

When you add or take away, the <u>first thing is</u> to **align the decimal points** and do the work.

Example:

- $0.5 + 0.2 = 0.7$

$$
\begin{array}{r}
0.5 \\
+\ 0.2 \\
\hline
0.7
\end{array}
$$

- $0.25 + 0.5 = 0.75$

$$
\begin{array}{r}
0.25 \\
+\ 0.50 \\
\hline
0.75
\end{array}
$$

- $1 - 0.4 = 0.6$

$$
\begin{array}{r}
1.0 \\
-\ 0.4 \\
\hline
0.6
\end{array}
$$

Practice 19

(1) 0.25 + 0.025 =   (2) 1.15 + 1.5 =

(3) 3 − 1.5 =   (4) 1.11 − 0.2 =

(5) 1 + 0.2 =   (6) 1 − 0.01 =

(7) 5 − (2.31 + 5.6) =   (8) 10 − 1.25 =

(9) 10 − (3.24 − 1.1) =   (10) 1 − 0.75 =

DECIMAL PLACES

Decimal place is the number of figures after the decimal point.

Example:

- (4 decimal places)
- 0.5 (1 decimal places)
- 0.500 (3 decimal places)

Practice 20

(1) Write 0.2 in 4 decimal places

(2) Write 3.142 into:

(a) 2 decimal places   (b) 1 decimal place

MULTIPLICATION OF DECIMALS

Total number of <u>decimal places before</u> is the <u>same</u> as the number of <u>decimal places after</u> multiplication.

Example

- ➤ 1.2 x 2 = 2.4 (1 decimal place)
- ➤ 1.234 x 2 = 2.468 (3 decimal places)
- ➤ 1.2 x 1.2 = 1.44 (2 decimal places)

Multiplying by 10, 100... – Every zero takes the decimal point one step **forward.**

Example:

- ➤ 1.32 x 10 = 13.2
- ➤ 1.32 x 100 = 132
- ➤ 1.32 x 1000 = 1320

Multiplying by 20, 300... – First, multiply by number (2 or 3) then add back zero(s).

Example

> ➢ $4 \times 30 = (4 \times 3)0 = 120$
> ➢ $20 \times 700 = (2 \times 7)000 = 14{,}000$

Practice 21

Work out the following:

(1) $1.2 \times 5 =$

(2) $1.1 \times 1.1 =$

(3) $8.95 \times 10 =$

(4) $8.95 \times 1000 =$

(5) $2.211 \times 30 =$

(6) $1.2 \times 600 =$

DIVISION OF DECIMALS

➢ **Dividing by digit** – Leave decimal point at the same place.

Example:

Work out the following:

➢ (1) $\frac{2.4}{2} \rightarrow \frac{2.4}{2} = 1.2$

➢ (2) $\frac{48.4}{4} \rightarrow \frac{48.4}{4} = 12.1$

➢ $\frac{1.2}{3} \rightarrow \frac{1.2}{3} = 0.4$

➢ **Dividing by 10, 100...** – Every zero takes the decimal point one step **backward.**

Example

➢ $\frac{2.5}{10} = = 0.25$

➢ $\frac{2.5}{100} = 0.025$

➢ $\frac{36}{100} = 0.36$

CHANGING DECIMAL INTO FRACTION

Change the following decimal numbers into fractions:

(a) 0.5   (b) 0.02   (c) 1.5

Answer

(a) $0.5 = \frac{5}{10} = [\frac{5 \div 5}{10 \div 5}] = \frac{1}{2}$

(b) $0.02 = \frac{2}{100} = \frac{1}{50}$

(c) $1.5 = \frac{15}{10} = \frac{3}{2}$

Dividing by 20, 300...

Example

$\quad\quad \ge \quad \frac{46.8}{20} = \frac{4.68}{2} = 2.34$

$\quad\quad \ge \quad \frac{1.32}{30} = \frac{0.135}{3} = 0.045$

- Given that: 15 x 15 = 225

    Work out 1.5 x 1.5

Answer

1.5 x 1.5 = $\frac{15}{10}$ x $\frac{15}{10}$ = $\frac{15 \times 15}{100}$ = $\frac{225}{100}$ = 2.25

Practice 22

(1) Change the following decimals into fractions: (a)0.4 =   (b)0.6 =   (c)0.9 =

Work out the following:

(2) $\frac{2.36}{2}$ =

(3) $\frac{0.136}{3}$ =

(4) $\frac{44.6}{10}$ =

(5) $\frac{44.56}{1000}$ =

(6) $\frac{44.6}{20}$ =

(7) $\frac{0.136}{30}$ =

(8) Which of the following is equal to 1.5 x 1.5?

(a) $\frac{15 \times 15}{10}$

(b) $\frac{15 \times 15}{100}$

(c) $\frac{15 \times 15}{1000}$

45

(9) Which of the following is <u>NOT</u> equal to 3.6?

(a) $\frac{36}{10}$ (b) $\frac{36 \times 3}{30}$ (c) $\frac{12 \times 3}{10}$ (d) $\frac{36}{100}$

(9) Given that: 354 x 95 = 33630

     Work out 35.4 x 9.5

PERCENTAGES

Per means **divide**, **Cent** means **100**

Therefore, **percent means divide by 100.**

Example:

$100\% = \frac{100}{100} = 1$

$20\% = \frac{20}{100} = 0.2$

- **"of" means "x"**

Example:

- 10% of 500 means $\frac{10}{100}$ x $500 = 50$
- 2% of £1000 = $\frac{2}{100}$ x £$1000 = £20$
- The game costs £50 before Christmas. After Christmas it will be discounted by 30%. What will be the sale price after Christmas?

A) **Sale price** = **Original price – Discount**

$$= £50 – 30\% \text{ of } £50$$

$$= £50 - \frac{30}{100} \; x \; £50$$

$$= £50 – £15 = £35$$

➢ £20 increased by 30%

$$= £20 + 30\% \text{ of } £20$$

$$= £20 + \frac{30}{100} \; x \; £20$$

$$= £20 + £6 = \underline{£26}$$

PERCENTAGE OF ONE ITEM IN A GROUP.

$$Percentage \; of \; item = \frac{Number \; of \; items}{Total \; items} \; x \; 100\%$$

Example:

➢ There are 50 students in the class: 20 boys and 30 girls. What are the percentage of boys and girls in the class?

Answer

Percentage of boys $= \dfrac{Number\ of\ boys}{Total\ number} \times 100\%$

$= \dfrac{20}{50} \times 100\% = 40\%$

Percentage of girls $= \dfrac{Number\ of\ girls}{Total\ number} \times 100\%$

$= \dfrac{30}{50} \times 100\% = 60\%$

[Total percent (40% + 60%) should be equal to 100%]

➢ There were 11,000 women in a village which make 55% of the village population. How many villagers were there?

Answer

Let the number of villagers be V

So, 55% of V = 11,000 $[\dfrac{55}{100} \times V = 11,000]$

→ V = $\dfrac{11,000 \times 100}{55}$ = 20,000

CHANGING PERCENTAGE INTO FRACTION

➢ $50\% = \dfrac{50}{100} = [\dfrac{50 \div 50}{100 \div 50}] = \dfrac{1}{2}$

➢ $25\% = \dfrac{25}{100} = [\dfrac{25 \div 25}{100 \div 25}] = \dfrac{1}{4}$

CHANGING PERCENTAGE INTO DECIMAL

➢ $50\% = \dfrac{50}{100} = 0.5$

➢ $25\% = \dfrac{25}{100} = 0.25$

CHANGING INTO PERCENTAGE [Just x 100]

Fraction into percentage

➢ $\dfrac{1}{4} = \dfrac{1}{4} \; x \; 100\% = 25\%$

Decimal into percentage

➢ $0.2 = 0.2 \times 100\% = 20\%$

50

Practice 27

(1) Fill in the following table:

Fraction	Decimal	Percentage
		20%
	0.85	
$\dfrac{1}{100}$		

Work out the following:

(2) $\dfrac{20}{100} \times 50 =$ (3) 2% of 60 million

(4) 25% of £500 =   (5) 5% of 50litre =

(6) 50 decreased by 20% =

(7) 40 has increased by 5% =

(5) Place <, > or =to make the following statement correct.

    (a) 50% of 400   10% of £2,500

(b) 5% of 3,300   20% of £850

(c) 30% of 10,000   5% of 60,000

(6) There were 60 million people in the

country of which 40% were men.

How many women were there?

(7) In 1665, 75,000 people (30%) of London

population died of plague.

What was the population in London?

(8) Math students have been asked which

transportation they use to go to school.

Here is the result:

Type of transportation	Number of students
Bus	24
Car	12
Walk	13

Tax	1

What percentage of the student use bus as their means of transportation?

5. BODMAS AND THE SYSTEM
(Calculator is <u>NOT</u> allowed)

BODMAS

BODMAS, stands for **B**racket, **O**f, **D**ivision, **M**ultiplication, **A**ddition and **S**ubtraction, explains the order of operation to solve an arithmetic expression.

<u>Example</u>: $1 + 2 \times 3 = 1 + 6 = 7$ [**M** then **A**]

Parentheses can be used for clarification.

$1 + (2 \times 3) = 1 + 6 = 7$

$(1 + 2) \times 3 = 3 \times 3 = 9$

➢ If you multiply the numbers you can cancel out. Eg. $\dfrac{12 \times 2}{6} = \dfrac{\cancel{12}^2 \times 2}{\cancel{6}^1} = 4$

➢ If you add up or subtract fractions you can't cancel out. Eg. $\dfrac{12+2}{6} = \dfrac{14}{6}$

Analyze the examples below:

➢ $\dfrac{20 \times 30}{60} = \dfrac{\cancel{20}^{10} \times \cancel{30}^1}{\cancel{60}^2} = 10$

$$\blacktriangleright \quad \frac{20+30}{60} = \frac{50}{60} = \frac{5}{6}$$

Practice 7

Work out the following:

(1) 2 + 3 x 4 =

(2) (2 + 3) x 4 =

(3) 2 + (3 x 4) =

(4) $\frac{1}{2}$ x 3(0.1 + 0.3) =

(4) $\frac{30 \; x \; 40}{20}$ =

(5) $\frac{30+40}{20}$ =

(6) 5 − (0.3 x 4) =

(6) $\frac{1}{2}$ x 7($\frac{6}{5}$ + $\frac{4}{5}$) =

(7) 20(1 − 0.4) =

(8) $\frac{40}{1-0.2}$ + 50 =

(9) $\frac{1.2+1.2}{0.2}$ =

(10) $\frac{1.2 \; x \; 1.4}{0.2}$ =

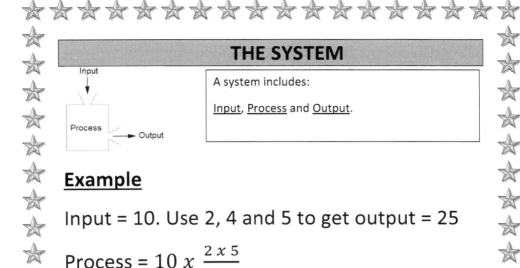

THE SYSTEM

A system includes:

Input, Process and Output.

Example

Input = 10. Use 2, 4 and 5 to get output = 25

Process = $10 \times \dfrac{2 \times 5}{4}$

Output = 25

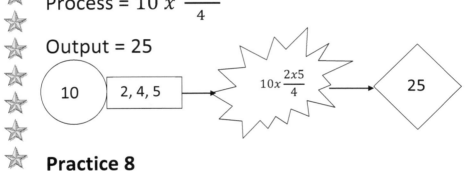

Practice 8

Write down the <u>process</u> for the following system.

(1)

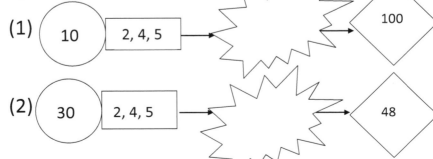

(2)

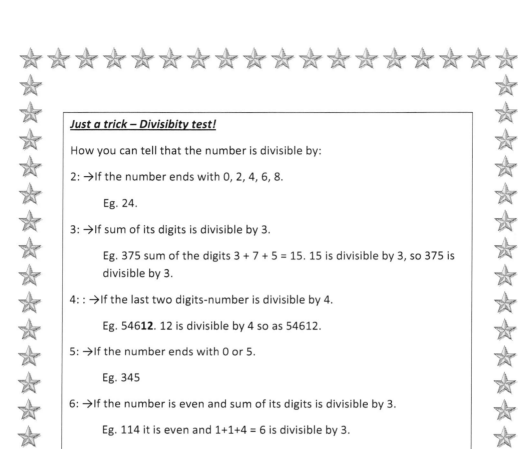

Just a trick – Divisibity test!

How you can tell that the number is divisible by:

2: →If the number ends with 0, 2, 4, 6, 8.

     Eg. 24.

3: →If sum of its digits is divisible by 3.

     Eg. 375 sum of the digits 3 + 7 + 5 = 15. 15 is divisible by 3, so 375 is divisible by 3.

4: : →If the last two digits-number is divisible by 4.

     Eg. 546**12**. 12 is divisible by 4 so as 54612.

5: →If the number ends with 0 or 5.

     Eg. 345

6: →If the number is even and sum of its digits is divisible by 3.

     Eg. 114 it is even and 1+1+4 = 6 is divisible by 3.

7: →Take the last digit off the number. Double it. Subtract the doubled number from the remaining number. If the result is divisible by 7 so as the whole number.

     Eg.175. 5x2=10. Then 17-10=7.

     So 175 is divisible by 7.

8: →If the last three-digit number is divisible by 8.

     Eg. 3**816**. 816 is divisible by 8 so as 3816.

9:→ If the sum of its digits is divisible by 9.

     Eg. 432. 4+3+2 = 9 is divisible by 9 so 432.

6. RATIOS AND PROPORTIONS

The <u>ratio of A to B is 2 : 1</u> means;

$$\frac{A}{B} = 2 \qquad \text{Or} \qquad A = 2B \text{ (A is twice of B)}$$

<u>Example</u> Consider the line below:

The ratio of AB to BC is 3:1. If BC = 4cm.

Find (a) AB (b) AC

<u>Answer</u>

$$\frac{AB}{BC} = 3 \qquad \rightarrow AB = 3BC$$

$$\rightarrow AB = 3 \text{ X } 4cm = \underline{12cm}$$

AC = AB + BC = 12cm + 4cm = <u>16cm</u>

<u>Example</u>

Consider the two lines below:

The length AB is one tenth of the length PQ.
Find the length AB.

Answer

$AB = \frac{1}{10} \ of \ PQ = \frac{1}{10} \ x \ 120cm = 12cm$

MODELS

Models use ratios. A model is something smaller made to be like a real thing.

Eg. A model of a house.

Lengths of the model and the corresponding lengths of the real thing have the **same ratio**.

Example

> ➢ The football pitch has a length 120m and width 40m. The model of the pitch has length 6cm.
> How long is the width of the model?

Answer

$$\frac{width\ of\ model}{lenght\ of\ model} = \frac{width\ of\ football\ pitch}{length\ of\ football\ pitch}$$

$$\frac{width\ of\ model}{6cm} = \frac{40cm}{120cm}$$

$$width\ of\ model = \frac{40cm}{120cm}\ x\ 6cm = 2cm$$

PROPORTIONS

(Amount of one component in a **mixture**)

Consider the box below:

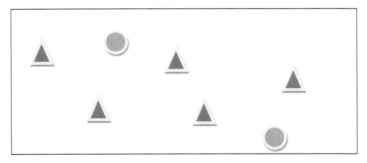

There are 7 shapes in total.

→ The proportion of the circles is <u>2 in 7</u>.

→ The proportion of the triangles is <u>5 in 7</u>.

- Proportion is just like equation – you can **multiply or divide both sides by the same number without changing the meaning**.

Example

Proportion if a the circle is 2 in 7 or

$$8 \text{ in } 28 \text{ [both x 4]}$$

$$4 \text{ in } 14 \text{ [both ÷ 2]}$$

Practice 28

(1) Consider the line below:

P   Q   R

The ratio of PQ to QR is 4.

a) If QR = 100m. Find PR.
b) If PQ =20km. Find PR.
c) If PR = 150cm. Find PQ and QR.

(2)

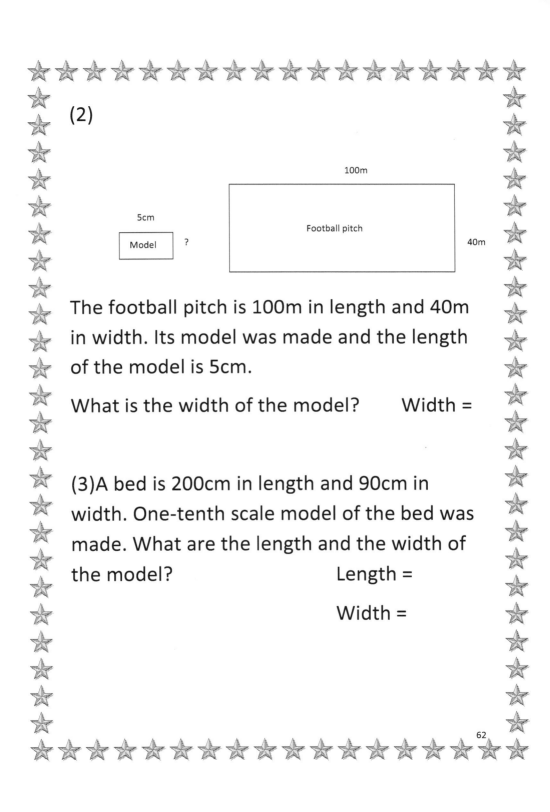

5cm

Model

?

100m

Football pitch

40m

The football pitch is 100m in length and 40m in width. Its model was made and the length of the model is 5cm.

What is the width of the model?   Width =

(3)A bed is 200cm in length and 90cm in width. One-tenth scale model of the bed was made. What are the length and the width of the model?   Length =

Width =

(4) In every 200millilitres of a drink there is 15g of sugar.

(a) How many grams of sugar in 100millilitres?

(b) How many grams of sugar in 1 litre?

(c) If I need 30g of sugar, how much volume of drink I should get?

7. ROUNDING

- If the number you are rounding is followed by $\underline{0}$, $\underline{1}$, $\underline{2}$, $\underline{3}$ and $\underline{4}$, **round down**.

Example: $2.\underline{1} \approx 2$ $20.\underline{4} \approx 20$

- If the number you are rounding is followed by $\underline{5}$, $\underline{6}$, $\underline{7}$, $\underline{8}$ and $\underline{9}$, **round up**.

Example: $104.\underline{5} \approx 105$ $9.\underline{9} \approx 10$

ROUND TO THE NEAREST **DIGITS**

(Digits are: **1, 2, 3, 4, 5, 6, 7, 8, 9**)

➢ $6.\underline{4} \approx 6$ $1.\underline{8} \approx 2$

➢ $3\frac{1}{10} - 1\frac{9}{10} = 3.1 - 1.9 \approx 3 - 2 = 1$

ROUND TO THE NEAREST **TENS**

(Tens are: **10, 20, 30, 40, 50, 60, 70, 80, 90**)

➢ $1\underline{4} \approx 10$ $2\underline{9} \approx 30$

ROUND TO THE NEAREST **HUNDREDS**

(Hundreds are: **100, 200, 300, 400, ...900**)

> $1\underline{4}9 \approx 100$ $4\underline{5}8 \approx 500$

ROUND TO THE NEAREST **THOUSANDS**

(Thousands are: **1,000, 2,000, 3,000, ...9,000**)

> $1,\underline{2}34 \approx 1,000$ $2,\underline{5}83 \approx 3,000$

ROUND TO THE NEAREST **TEN THOUSANDS**

(Ten thousands are: **10,000, 20,000, ...90,000**)

> $1\underline{2},912 \approx 10,000$ $4\underline{8},123 \approx 50,000$

ROUND TO THE NEAREST **MILLION**

(Millions are: **1,000,000, 2,000,000...**)

> $7,\underline{2}34,567 \approx 7,000,000$
> $2,\underline{8}13,423 \approx 3,000,000$

Practice 29

(1) Round to the nearest <u>digits</u>:

    (a)1.9 ≈   (b)6.1 ≈   (c)4.8 ≈

(2) Round to the nearest <u>tens</u>:

    (a)69   (b)72   (c)51

(3) Round to the nearest <u>hundreds</u>:

    (a)145   (b)360   (c)930

(4)Round to the nearest <u>thousands</u>:

    (a)2,500   (b)5,450   (c)4,500

(5)Round to the nearest <u>ten thousands</u>:

    (a)14,589   (b)84,912   (c)68,312

(6) Round to the <u>nearest millions</u>:

 (a)1,512,413 (2)8,435,978 (c)6,645,314

(7)Work out the <u>approximate</u> value of

$4\frac{8}{10} - 1\frac{2}{9} + 2\frac{4}{5} \approx$

(8)

	Round 49,467
To the nearest 10,000	
To the nearest 1,000	
To the nearest 100	

8. ALGEBRA

- **ALGEBRAIC OPERATION**
- **EXPRESSIONS**
- **EQUATIONS**

ALGEBRAIC OPERATION

In Algebra, letters and symbols represent numbers.

Example:

A + 2 = 5. (This means that A =3). Or

X + Y = 4 (X and Y are the set of numbers

whose sum is 4). So X and Y can be:

(0 and 4), (1 and 3) or (2 and 2).

Test yourself

Given that X + Y = 6. The value of X or Y is less than 4. What the values of X and Y could be?

Answer 3,3

SIMPLIFY

To simplify the expression means to put it in its simplest form. This includes to put **like term** together. **Unlike terms** do not add up together.

a and a are like terms; so a + a = 2a

a and A are unlike terms so they can't add up.

Example

Addition and Subtraction

- ➢   a + a +b + a + b = 3a + 2b
- ➢   4a + 7b + 6a − 5b = 10a + 2b
- ➢   a + a = 2a [2a = 2 x a]

Multiplication and division

- ➢   10 x a = 10a
- ➢   a x a = a^2
- ➢   a x b = ab   [ab = a x b]
- ➢ $\frac{8a^2b}{4ab}$ = 2a   [The top and the bottom terms cancel]

➤ $\dfrac{2a \times 3b}{3a} = 2b$

➤ $\dfrac{2a+3b}{3a} = ?$ [can't be simplified any further]

Note:

A x B = B x A

A + B = B + A

The sign (+ or -) of the letter is written before the letter.

A – B = - B + A (A has + sign and B has – sign)

[+ sign is usually is omitted if the letter or number is at the beginning]

Practice 30

(1) Given the expression: x − y.

What are the signs of x and y?

(2) Simplify the following:

(a) a + a + a + a

(b) t + q + t + t − 2t + q + t + q

(c) 4m + 6n + 5m − 6n   (d) t x t

(e) −a + a   (f) $\dfrac{a}{a}$ (h) $\dfrac{9bc^2}{6abc}$

(i) $\dfrac{8ab \; x \; 2bc}{4abc}$

(3)

Tick whether the statement is True or False		
Statement	T	F
A + B = B + A		
A − B = B − A		
A x B = B x A		
A ÷ B = B ÷ A		

(4) Given that X + Y = 20. Find the sets of X and Y which are both prime numbers.

71

EXPAND AND SIMPLIFY

- To <u>expand</u> is to <u>remove the brackets</u>.
- The term which is outsidethe bracket is multiplied by <u>each</u> term in the bracket.

Example

➢ Expand: a(b + c)

a(b + c) = a x b + a x c = ab + ac

- To expand two brackets: <u>Each</u> term from one bracket is multiplied to <u>each</u> item in another bracket.

Example: Q)Expand (a + b)(c + d)

A) (a + b)(c + d) = a x c + a x d + b x c + b x d

= ac + ad + bc + bd

Q) Remove the brackets (a + 2)(a + 3)

A) (a + 2)(a + 3) = a x a + a x 3 + 2 x a + 2 x 3

$$= a^2 + 3a + 2a + 6$$

$$= a^2 + 5a + 6$$

FACTORIZE [The opposite of expand]

- Find the **common factor** (item) and keep it out of the bracket.

Example

Factorize:

(a) ab − ac   (b) 4p + 4pq   (c) $qr^2 + qr$

Answer

(a) ab − ac = a(b − c)   [a is a common factor]

(b) 4p + 4pq = 4p(1 + q)   [$4p$ is a common factor]

(c) $qr^2 + qr = qr(r + 1)$

Practice 31

(1) Expand the following and simplify if possible

(a) P(q + r)

(b) (p + q)(r + s)

(c) $(t + 1)(t + 2)$

(d) $(a + b)(c - d)$

(e) $(p + 2)(p - 4)$

(2) Factorize the following:

(a) $pq - pr$

(b) $8mn - 8n$

(c) $3abc + 3bc$

(d) $2abc - 4ac$

<u>Distributive law</u> → (a + b) x c = a x c + b x c

12 x 15 = (10 + 2) x 15 = 150 + 30 = 180

13 x 5 =

(10+ 3) x 5　　= 10 x 5 + 3 x 5

　　　　　　　　= 50 + 15 = 65

99 x 2 =

(100 − 1) x 2　= 100 x 2 − 1 x 2

　　　　　　　　= 200 − 2 = 198

<u>Associative law</u> → (a x b) x c = a x (b x c)

(2 x 3) x 4 = 2 x (3 x 4)

　　6 x 4 = 2 x 12

Test yourself

Work out the following:

(1)12 x 4 = (10 + 2) x 4 =

(2)97 x 5 = (100 − 3) =

(3)(3 x 4) x 5 = 3 x (4 x 5) =

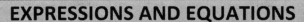

EXPRESSIONS AND EQUATIONS

- Example of **expression**: a + 2
- Example of **equation**: a + 2 = 10

Example

Let X and Y represents two numbers; then

Statement	Expression
Sum of two numbers	X + Y
Difference of two numbers	X – Y
Product of two numbers	XY

Example

Write down the expressions for the following statements (Let a as unknown number):

Statement:

I had £20 and I gave some money away.

Expression: £20 - a

Statement:

I had some money and I gave £50 away.

Expression: a - £50

Practice 33

Fill in the following table (let a be unknown):

Statement	Expression
I had some money and I gave £20 away	
I had some money and I gave half of money away	
I had some money and two third of my money away	
Ihad some money and i gave 20% of my money away	

EQUATIONS

$$40 = 8 + 4P$$

If you take an item to other side of the equation, the sign changes from:

(+) to (-)

(x) to (÷) and vice versa.

Example: $4 \times R + 8 = 40$

$$4 \times R = 40 - 8$$

$$R = \frac{40-8}{4} = \frac{32}{4} = 8$$

Example:

(1)Solve the equation x + 21 = 463

Answer

(to get x you need to move 21 to the right side. 21 has + sign, so at the other side will have − sign)

x + 21 = 463

→ x = 463 − 21

$$
\begin{array}{r}
4\quad 6\quad 3 \\
-\quad\ \ 2\quad 1 \\
\hline
4\quad 4\quad 2
\end{array}
$$

x = 463 − 21 = 442

(2)Solve the following equation:

$$D \times 5 = 250 \times 2$$

Answer

D x 5 = 250 x 2

$$\rightarrow D = \frac{250 \times 2}{5} = 100$$

Practice 34

Solve the following equations:

(1) x − 34 = 122

(2) m x 4 = 88

(3) $\frac{p}{20} = 50$

(4) $\frac{m \; x \; 5}{6} = 10$

(5) $1 + \frac{x}{2} = 3$

(6) $\frac{2x}{3} + \frac{1}{2} = \frac{5}{2}$

(7) x + y = 100. Find x if y = 21.

(8) Given that A = 8 + b.

Find the value of the expression $\frac{2}{3}$(A - B)

HOW TO MAKE EQUATIONS

Example:

You will be charged £1 to use printer. To print one coloured page it costs 15p. To print black and white page it costs 10p.

(a) Write the equation to calculate the **total cost of printing** (Let C be the number of coloured pages and B the number of black and white pages)

(b) How much will it cost to print 10 coloured pages?

(c) How much will it cost to print 20 coloured and 30 black and white pages?

Answer

(a) Total cost (£)= 1 + 0.1 x B + 0.15 x C

(b) Total cost (£) = 1.00 + 0.1 x 0 + 0.15 x 10

$$= \quad 1 + \quad 0 \quad + \quad 1.5 = 2.5$$

(c) Total cost (£) = 1 + 0.1 x 30 + 0.15 x 20

$$= 1 \quad + \quad 3 \quad + \quad 3 \quad = 7$$

GUESS MY NUMBER - *(make equation and solve)*

Q) I think a number. I multiply it by 6. Then I take away 35. The result is 37. Guess my number.

A) Let your number be a. Then

(a x 6) – 35 = 37

→ (a x 6) = 37 + 35 = 72

→ a = $\frac{72}{6}$ = 12. So your number is 12! *"Right?"*

Check: 12 x 6 – 35 = 37

Practice 35

<u>Answer</u> the following questions:

(1) Park entrance costs £8. Every ride in the park costs £4 per ride.

    (a) Let R be the number of ride, write down the formula for the total cost (C) to the park.

    (b) What is the total cost for 5 rides?

    (c) How many rides will you get for £40.

    (d) If you had £50, how many rides will you get and how much change will be left?

(2) I think a number. Multiply it by 7. Then add 50. The result is 890. What is the number?

TWO EQUATIONS

If you have two equations, you can <u>add</u>, <u>subtract</u>, <u>multiply</u> and <u>divide</u> them together.

Example

$$K = 9.......[\text{equation (i)}]$$

$$M = 3......[\text{equation (ii)}]$$

Then, $K = 9$

$+$ $\underline{M = 3}$

$K + M = 9 + 3 = 12$

Q) Find (a)$K - M$ (b)$K \times M$ (c)$K \div M$

A)(a)6 (b)27 (c)3

Try this!

$$X + Y = 12$$

$+$ $\underline{X - Y = 4}$

_____

<u>Answer</u>

$2X = 16 \rightarrow X = 8, Y = 4$

9. MEASUEREMENTS

TABLE OF UNITS
LENGTH
1 centimetre = 10 millimetres
1 metre = 100 centimetres
1 kilometre = 1000 metres
MONEY
£1 (pound) = 100p (pence)
WEIGHT
1 kilogram = 1000 gram
TIME
1 minute = 60 seconds
1 hour = 60 minutes
VOLUME
1 litre = 1000 millilitres

CONVERSIONS OF UNITS

Use **CROSS MULTIPLICATION** to convert units.

Example:

If $A = B$

$C = ?$ Then **A x ? = B x C → ? = $\frac{B \times C}{A}$**

Use the table of units above

Length

1 metre (m) = 100 centimetre (cm)

- To change m to cm, just <u>multiply by 100</u>.
  Example
  ➤   <u>2 m</u> = [2 x 100] = <u>200 cm</u>
  ➤   <u>1.5 m</u> = [1.5 x 100] = <u>150 cm</u>
- To convert cm to m, <u>divide by 100</u>.

  Example

  ➤   <u>250 cm</u> = [$\frac{250}{100}$] = <u>2.5 m</u>

  Fill in the blanks

  ➤   1 m + 60 cm = _____ m

$$\underline{1\ m + 60\ cm} = [1\ m + \frac{60}{100}] = \underline{1.6\ m}$$

➤   0.4 m + 50 cm = _____ cm

0.4 m + 50 cm = [0.4 x 100 cm + 50 cm]

= 40 cm + 50 cm = $\underline{90\ cm}$

➤   5mile = 8km.

How many miles is 320km?

Answer

5mile   =   8km

?mile   =   320km, then

?mile x 8km = 5mile x 320km

$$\rightarrow ?\ mile = \frac{5mile\ x\ \cancel{320km}^{40}}{\cancel{8km}^{1}} = 200 miles$$

➤   One quarter of 1 kg = $\frac{1}{4}\ x\ 1kg$

=0.25kg = 250g

Practice 36

(1) 16 feet = 5 metres

How many metres is 6 feet?

(2) 150 millilitres of water is flowing from the tap in every 5 seconds.
How many <u>litres</u> of water flows in:
(a) Every minute?
(b) Every hour?

10. SHAPES

- **2D SHAPES → AREAS AND PERIMETERS**
- **3D SHAPES → VOLUME AND SURFACE AREA**
- **LINES OF SYMETRY**

2D SHAPES

- ***3 SIDED SHAPE - TRIANGLE***

4 types of triangles are:

1) **Equilateral triangle**
2) **Isosceles triangle**
3) **Right angled triangle**
4) **Scalene triangle**

1) **Equilateral triangle** - all side are equal and all angles are equal.

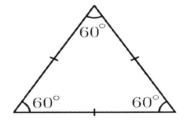

89

2) **<u>Isosceles triangle</u>** - two lines are equal and two angles (**base angles**) are equal.

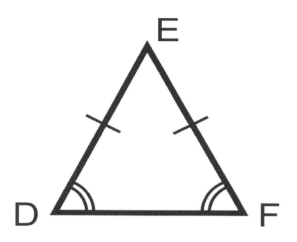

3) **<u>Right angled triangle</u>** - one of its angle is right angle(90^0).

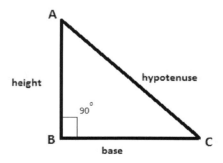

4) **Scalene triangle** - all lines and angles are different.

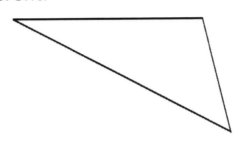

Practice 37

(1) Match the triangle and its property.

Types of triangle		Properties
Scalene triangle		All angles are equal
Right angled triangle		All angles are different
Isosceles triangle		One angle is 90°
Equilateral triangle		Two angles are equal

- The sum of the angle of triangle is always = 180°

(2) Can right angled triangle be:

(a) Isosceles triangle?

(b) Equilateral triangle? Explain.

- **_4-SIDED SHAPES_**

Square

Square has **4 sides** which are **all equal** and 4 angles which are **all 90⁰.**

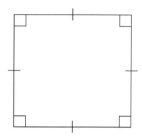

Rectangle

Rectangle has 4 sides of which two sides are equal and all 4 angles are 90⁰.

• *POLYGONS*

A polygon is any two-dimensional shape formed with straight lines.

Table below show the names of polygons:

TABLE OF **POLYGONS**	
Number of **sides**	**Name** of polygon
3	**Tri**angle
4	**Quadri**lateral
5	**Penta**gon
6	**Hexa**gon
7	**Hepta**gon
8	**Octa**gon
9	**Nona**gon
10	**Deca**gon

Polygon can be regular or irregular.

Example

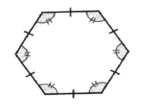 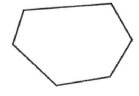

- **Cycle**

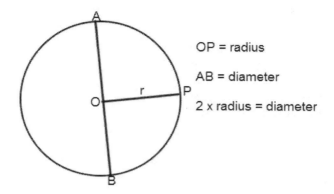

OP = radius

AB = diameter

2 x radius = diameter

5) **Centre** (o)is the middle of the circle.

6) **Radius** is the line from the centre to the circle (circumference).

7) **Diameter** is the line from one end of a circle, passing through the centre than touch the other side of the circle.

So **diameter = 2 x radius**

That is if radius = 5cm, then

Diameter = 2 x 5cm = 10cm

The size of a circle is determined by its radius.

AREAS AND PERIMETERS

Area is a space covered by the shape.

The units of area are: unit is m^2, cm^2, km^2...

Perimeter is the length of path that surrounds the shape. Its unit is m, cm, km...

Every shape has its own formula to find its area and perimeter.

Square

Consider the square with side length L.

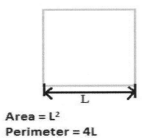

Area = L^2
Perimeter = 4L

Example:: Calculate the area of the square whose sides are 9cm.

Area = 9cm x 9cm = <u>81cm^2</u>

Rectangle

The rectangle with length l and width w has:

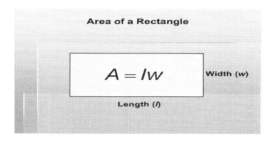

Area = l x w and **Perimeter = 2(l + w)**

Example: (1)

Find the area and perimeter of the rectangle below:

2 cm

5 cm

Answer

Area = l x w = 5 cm x 2 cm = 10 cm^2

Perimeter = 2(l + w) = 2(5 + 2) = 14 cm

Example: (2)

Find the area and perimeter of the figure below:

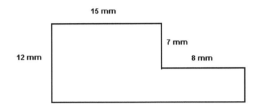

Answer

Cut the figure into two shapes. Then find the areas separately and then add them together.

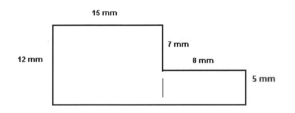

Area = 15 x 12 + 8 x 5 = 15 x (10 + 2) + 40

$\qquad$ = 150 + 30 + 40 = 150 + 70 = 220cm^2

Perimeter = 12 + 15 + 7 + 8 + 5 + (8+15)=70cm

Example: (3)

Calculate the shaded area in the figure below:

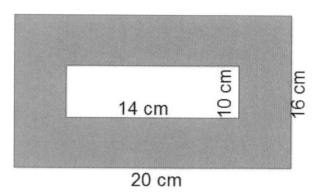

Answer

Shaded area = outer area − inner area

= 20cm x 16cm − 10cm x 14cm

= 320cm^2 − 140cm^2

= 180cm^2

Example: (4)

 EQUAL PERIMETER

Area of square = ?

The perimeter of the regular pentagon is equal to the perimeter of the square. If the side of the pentagon is 4cm. Calculate the area of the square.

Answer

Perimeter of the pentagon = 5 x 4cm =20cm

Perimeter of the square = 4L = 20cm

→ L = 20cm/4 = 5cm

So, the area of the square = L^2 = 5^2 = 25cm^2

3D SHAPES

3D Shapes and surface areas

Sphere – Has one <u>curved</u> surface area.

Cylinder– Has three surface areas:

Two ends <u>circular</u> and one <u>curved</u> surface areas.

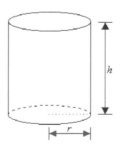

Cone– Has two surface areas: One <u>curved</u> one <u>circular</u>.

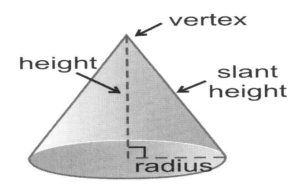

Cube– Has six similar <u>square</u> surface areas.

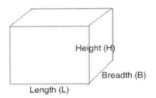

Cuboids– Has six <u>rectangular</u> surface areas.

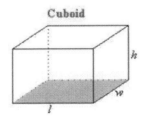

Prism – Has five surface areas:

Two <u>triangular</u> and three <u>rectangular</u> surface areas.

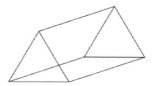

Pyramid– Has five surface areas:

Four <u>triangular</u> and one <u>square/recta</u>ngle surface areas

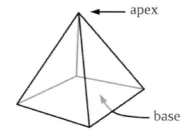

Line of symmetry is the line which cut the shape into <u>exactly two halves</u>.

Example: The (equilateral) triangle below has three lines of symmetry.

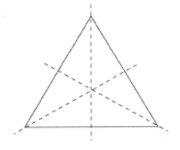

Practice 38

(1) Find the area and perimeter of the following figure:

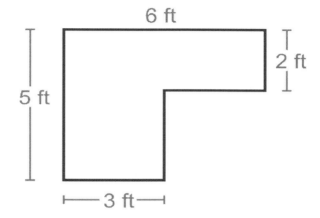

6 ft

2 ft

5 ft

3 ft

(2) Calculate the shaded area in the figure below:

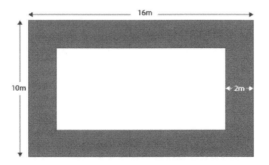

16m

10m

2m

(3) The perimeter of the regular hexagon is equal to the perimeter of the square. If the side of the hexagon is 6cm. Calculate the area of the square.

(4) How many lines of symmetry do the following figures have?

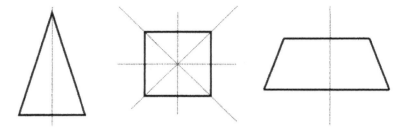

- **TYPES OF ANGLES**
- **ESTIMATING ANGLES**

An angle is formed when two lines meet.

TYPES OF ANGLES

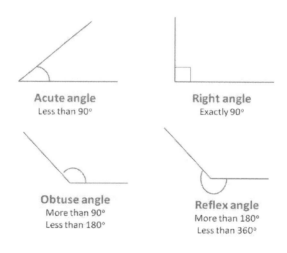

Acute angle
Less than 90°

Right angle
Exactly 90°

Obtuse angle
More than 90°
Less than 180°

Reflex angle
More than 180°
Less than 360°

ESTIMATING THE ANGLES

90° (right angle) is formed when two lines meet **perpendicularly**.

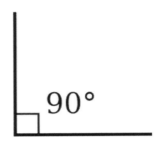

Since you know the size of 90°, you can <u>estimate</u> the sizes of other angles.

Example

45° = 90° ÷ 2

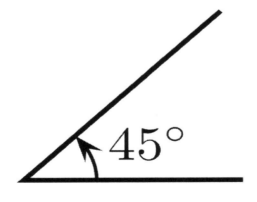

30° = 90° ÷ 3

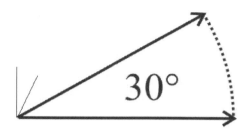

120° = 90° + 30°

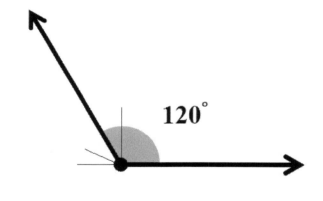

Practice 39

(1) Estimate (draw) the angles:

(a) 150° (90 + 60)
(b) 270° (90 + 90 + 90)
(c) 315° (90 + 90 + 90 + 45)

(2) Estimate the following angles:

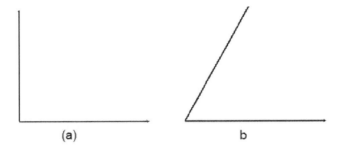

(a)   b

(3) A pizza was cut three times as follows:

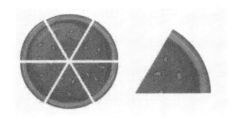

How many degrees is one slice of pizza?

(4) Mario was walking towards North and he changed his direction to where he was coming from.

How many degrees did he turn?

12. CO-ORDINATES

- X – Y AXIS
- LINES AND POINTS
- TRANSFORMATION

X – Y AXIS

X – axis – horizontal axis.

Y – axis – vertical axis

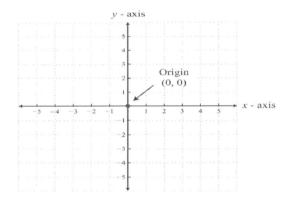

When reading points, <u>first read x-axis then y-axis</u>. So the co-ordinate (2, 3) means x=2, y=3.

(x, y)

Example: At point M; (x = 2, y = 1.5)

Test yourself

At point L; (x = ____, y = ____)

At point N; (x = ____, y = ____)

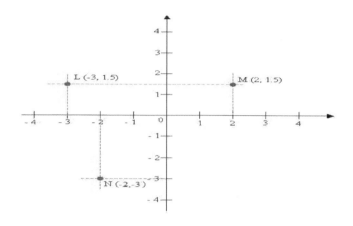

Practice 40

A) What is the co-ordinates of the points A, B, C and D in the figure below?

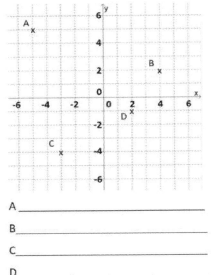

A _____

B _____

C _____

D _____

B) On the axis below, mark the points: (5,5), (-4,1), (-3,-2)and (5,-5).

LINES AND POINTS

Example: (1)

In t $_{cm}$ figure below <u>line AB = 4cm</u>.

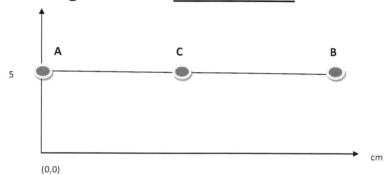

Point C is the **midpoint** of the line AB. Point A lays on y = 5 Write down the co-ordinates of the points A, B and C.

Answer

Point A(x = 0, y = 5)

Point B(x = 4, y = 5)

Point C(x = 2, y = 5)   [x = 4/2 = 2]

Example: (2)

In the figure below line AB = 4cm.

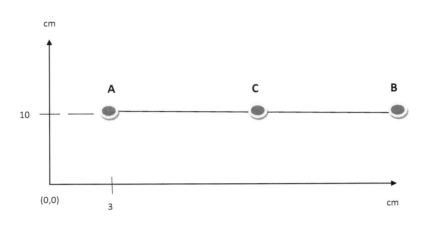

Point C is the midpoint of the line AB. Write down the co-ordinates of the points A, B and C.

Answer

Point A(x = 3, y = 10)

Point B(x = 7, y = 10)   [x = 3 + 4 = 7]

Point C(x = 5, y = 10)   [x = 4/2+3 = 5]

Practice 41

(1) In the figure below line AB = 6cm. Point
C is the midpoint of the line AB. Write
down the co-ordinates of the points A, B
and C.

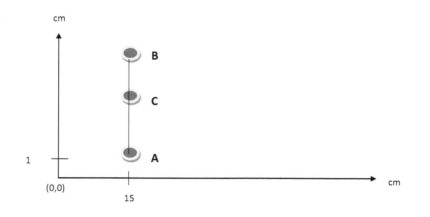

Point A(x = ___, y = ___)

Point B(x = ___, y = ___)

Point C(x = ___, y = ___)

(2) Consider the figure below. ABCD is a square of sides = 8cm. O is the centre of the square. Write down the co-ordinates of the points A, B, C, D and O.

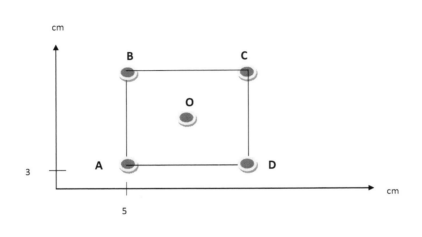

A(x = ___, y = ___)

B(x = ___, y = ___)

C(x = ___, y = ___)

D(x = ___, y = ___)

O(x = ___, y = ___)

TRANSFORMATION

Transformation is when a shape(points) transforms (changes) to another place.

TYPES OF TRANSFORMATION

Reflection

Translation

- ### *Reflection*

The point can be **reflected** to the same distance from any **mirror line**.

Example:

The points A, B and C of a triangle are reflected on the line Y-AXIS to the points E, D and F.

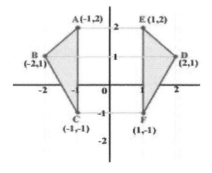

- *__Translation__*

Translation is to moving the point or shape into different position. The **two** movements can be (1) **Left or Right** (2) **Up or Down**.

__Example__

The vertexes of the triangle below translated:

Two steps to the **right** and **three** steps **up**.

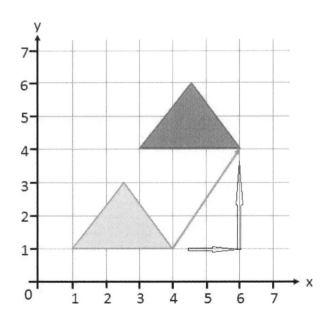

Practice 42

(1) Consider the diagram below:

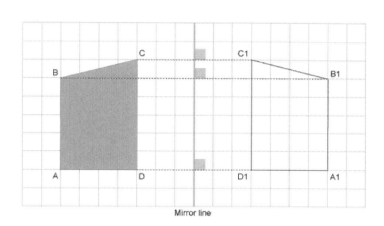

Mirror line

Which statement explains the diagram?

(a) Reflected on the x-axis
(b) Translated six steps to the right and one step up
(c) Reflected on the mirror line y-axis

(2) Consider the diagram below:

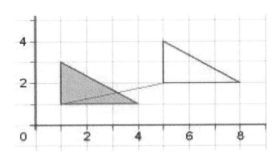

Which statement explains the diagram?

(a) Reflected on the x-axis
(b) Translated four steps to the right and one step up
(c) Reflected on the mirror line y-axis

13. HANDLING DATA

Handling data passes three processes:

(1) **Collect** data. Either collect it yourself (**primary data**) or use internet, books etc. (**secondary data**)

(2) **Organize** the data (eg. On **table, bar chart, pictogram, pie chart** etc.).

(3) **Analyse** the data (eg. Find **mean, median, mode, range** etc.).

DATA COLLECTION

- ***Primary data and secondary data***
  - ❖ **Primary data**

Data that you collected it *yourself*.

Eg. If you count the number of cars.

  - ❖ **Secondary data**

Data that was collected by someone else.

Eg. If you read from internet.

- *Discrete data and continuous data*
  - ❖ **Discrete data**

Can only be an **integer** (a whole number).

Example: Number of student, say 23 and not 23.5.

- ❖ **Continuous data**

Can take **any value** (decimal point).

Example: Weight of the student in the class, say 32.4 kg.

- *Single data and grouped data*
  - ❖ **Single Data**

Represent one entry.

Example

Marks of students in a class of 10 pupils.

40, 50, 50, 30, 60, 80, 70, 70, 70, 90.

- ❖ **Grouped Data**

Represent group entries.

Example: of grouped data:

1 – 100
101 – 200...

DATA ORGANIZATION

Data can be represented as:

- Table
- Bar chart
- Pictogram
- Pie chart

Practice 43

Table

Consider the table below:

Type of Pet	Tally	Frequency
Dog	ⅢⅡ ⅢⅡ ‖	12
Cat	ⅢⅡ ‖	7
Goldfish	ⅢⅡ ǀ	6
Budgie	‖‖	3
Hamster	‖	2
Lizard	ǀ	1
Snake	ǀ	1
Rabbit	‖‖	3

(a) Which is the most popular pet?

(b) How many pets are there all together?

(2) The weights of 10 students in kg are:

39.5, 40.8, 41.5, 44.5, 45.3, 46.5, 44.5,

46.5, 50.1, 44.5

Record the information in the table below:

Mass in kg	Number of students
35 – 40	
40 – 45	
45 – 50	
50 – 55	
Total	

Bar chart

Consider the bar chart below

  (a) How many pears are there?

  (b) How many more apples than oranges?

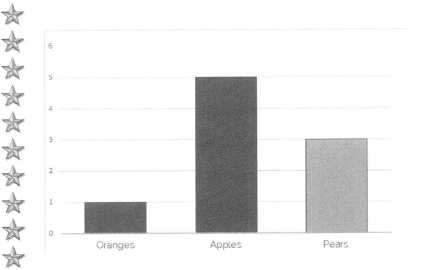

Pictogram

Consider the pictogram below:

    (a) How many children chose cottage pie?

    (b) How many children chose roast dinner?

Note:

One circle represents two children.

So, half a circle represents one child.

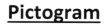 = 2 children	
What we would like for our school lunches!	
Vegetable lasagne	●● ◖
Chicken pie	●●●●●●
Cheese salad	●●●● ◖
Cottage pie	● ◖
Casserole	●●●●●● ◖
Roast dinner	●●●●●●●●

Pie chart

The sum of the angle of the pie chart = 360°

Example: 90° + 90° + 120° + 60° = 180°

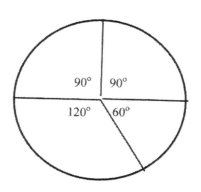

(5)**Pi chart**

Yussuf, Yazid, Cabral and Hafidh established a business and they agreed to share the profit as shown in the pie chart below.

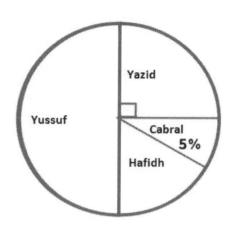

(a) How many degrees does Hafidh sector represent?

(b) Last month, they shared a business profit of £21,600. How much did each get?

DATA ANALYSES

Mean, Median, Mode and Range

Mean is the average $= \dfrac{sum\ of\ values}{number\ of\ values}$

Example:

Five numbers were given: 7, 3, 2, 6, 7

Mean $= \dfrac{7+3+2+6+7}{5} = \dfrac{25}{5} = 5$

Median is the middle number (after arranging the numbers in order.

Arranging in order; the numbers will be:

$$2, 3, 6, 7, 7$$

So the Median (middle number) is 6.

Mode is the number which occur the most.

So Mode = 7

Range = Highest number – Lowest number

$= 7 - 2 = 5$

Practice 44

(1) Given the numbers: 15, 12, 11, 12, 10.

Find the mean, median, mode and range of the numbers.

(2) I bought two tickets for £4 and £6. What is the mean cost of the tickets? Then I bought another ticket for £6. What is the total average cost of the tickets?

QUESTION BANK

(1)3419 + 76 =

(2)7 – 12 =

(3)4635 – 783 =

(4)132 x 12 =

(5)The first two terms of the series are:

1, 4, ___, ___, ___. The series follow the

Rule: x2 then +2. Find the third term, fourth

term and fifth term.

Work out the following:

(6)864 ÷ 27 =

(7)Find the HCF of 20 and 30.

(8)Find the LCM of 4 and 5.

(9)Find the prime factorization of 150.

(10)Simplify: $\dfrac{140}{2100}$

Work out the following:

(11) $\frac{4}{5} + \frac{5}{6} =$

(12) $1\frac{3}{4} - \frac{5}{6} =$

(13) $\frac{15}{16} \div \frac{12}{8} =$

(14) $1\frac{1}{2} + 1\frac{1}{4} =$

(15) $1 - \frac{5}{7} =$

(16) $1 + \frac{2}{100} =$

Fill in the missing number

(17) $\frac{15}{18} = \frac{5}{}$

(18) Given that: 325 x 12 = 3900

Find the values of: (a) 3.25 x 1.2 =

$\qquad$ (b) $32.5 \times \frac{12}{30} =$

(19) Work out: 1.2 x 400 =

(20) £50 decreased by 10% =

(21) Fill in the missing numbers.

Fraction	Decimal	Percentage
$\dfrac{4}{5}$		
	0.52	
		48%

(22) Consider the diagram below:

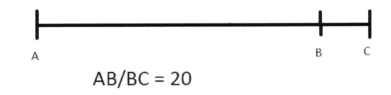

A   B   C

AB/BC = 20

The ratio of the distance AB:BC = 20.

BC = 70 cm.

Calculate the distance AC in metre.

(23) The model of the car has been drawn at a ratio of 1:100. (This means 1 cm of the drawing represent 100 cm of the real car).

The length of the model car is 2.5 cm. Then,

The length of the real car is _____ m.

(24)The bag of chocolate buttons contains <u>white chocolate buttons</u> and <u>brown chocolate buttons.</u>

In every 10 buttons, there are 6 white buttons.

The box contains 40 buttons.

How many (a) White chocolate buttons and

(b)Brown chocolate buttons are in the bag?

(25)

Round to the nearest	5,546,850
Millions	
Ten thousands	
Thousands	
Hundreds	

(26) Factorize: $15a^2b^2 - 18ab$

Expand the following:

(27) $(a + b)(a - b)$

(28) $(x + 2)(x - 3)$

(29) Solve the equation: $x - 483 = 568$

(30) Entrance to the fun fair cost £5. Each ride (r) costs £3. Each meal (m) costs £6.

    (a) Write down the equation foe the Total Cost TC(£).

I want to go on five rides and have two meals.

    (b) How much it will cost?

(31) Guess my number.

I think a number, n. Divide it by 4 and add 10. The result is 35.

(i) Which equation you can use to find my number?

(a)$n + \frac{10}{4} = 35$ (b)$\frac{n+10}{4} = 35$

(c)$\frac{n}{4} + 10 = 35$

(ii)What is the number?

(32)Given that: K = 12 + A and

M = 14 −A

The value of K + M =

(33) 10 feet = 3 yards

(a)How many yards is 6 feet?

(b)How many feet is 120 yards?

(34)

Quantity	Unit
Distance	Meter (m)
Time	Second (s)
Speed (distance/time)	Meter/second (m/s)

$$a = \frac{m}{m/s}$$

Which quantity does "a" represent?

(a)Distance   (b)Time   (c)Speed

(35)The perimeter of the square is 100m.

Find its area.

(36)The rectangle below has a perimeter =
48cm. Find its area. Area =

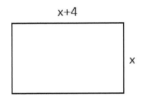

(37)Consider the diagram below:

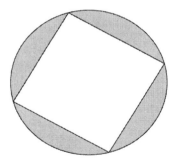

The area of a circle is 79 cm^2.

The sides of the square inside the circle has length = 7 cm.

Find the shaded area.

(38) The axes below are in cm.

Find the area and perimeter of the rectangle.

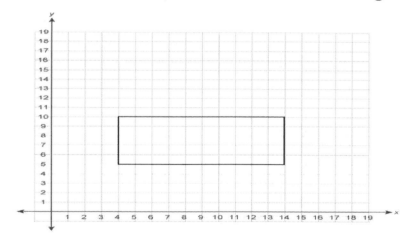

(39) Work out the following:

$$◊ + θ = 7$$

$$◊ - θ = 1$$

$$◊ =$$

$$θ =$$

(40)Work out the following:

$$\square \times \Delta = 200$$

$$\square \div \Delta = 2$$

$$\square + \Delta =$$

ANSWERS TO PRACTICES

Practice1

(1)(a)$4 - 6 = -2$ (b)$-10 + 5 = -5$ (c)$1 - 8 = -7$ (d)$-8 + 9 = 1$ (2)(a)825mls (b)-1°c

(3)(a) 1, 6, 11, 16, <u>21</u>, <u>26</u>, <u>31</u>   Rule: +5

(b) 20, 17, 14, <u>11</u>, <u>8</u>, <u>5</u>   Rule: -3

(c) 2, 8, 32, <u>128</u>, <u>512</u>, <u>2048</u>.   Rule: x4

4(a) Rule: x3, -1   Trend:1, 2,<u>5</u>, <u>14</u>, <u>41</u>

(b) Rule: -1, x3   Trend: 2, 3, <u>6</u>, <u>15</u>, <u>42</u>

Practice 2

(1)6658 (2)9355 (3)(a)368 (b)710 (c)460

(4)

	7	2	1	**7**	9
+		5	6	3	**2**
	7	7	8	1	1

Practice 4

(1)210000 (2)126 (3)126000 (4)90

Practice 5

(1)4797 (2)125 (3)97 (4)25

Practice 6

(1)5-(1.50+0.75+1.20)=£1.55 (2)32-21=11°c (3)$\frac{40}{4}$x0.95=£9.50 (4)5-($\frac{3}{2}$x2+x$\frac{3}{4}$1.6)=80p (5)(a)700x500=350,000 plants (b)350000x150= 52,500,000g (52.5 million grams)

Practice 7

(1)0 (2)20 (3)105 (4)4.21 (5)0.8

Practice 8

(1)$10x\frac{5x4}{2}$ (2)$30x\frac{2x4}{5}$

Practice 9

(1)(a)1,2,3,4,6,12 and 1,2,3,6,9,18 (b)1,2,3,6 (c)6 (2)12

Practice 10

(1)(a)3,6,9,12,15,18,21,34 and 4,8,12,16,20,24 (b)12, 24 (c)12 (2)20

Practice 11

(1)59 (2)20 (3)

Factors of 30	Multiples of 3	Prime numbers
1, 2, 3, 5, 6, 10, 15,	3, 6, 9, 12, 15	1, 3, 5, 7, 11, 13

(4)(a)2x2x2x5x5 (b)2x2x2x3x5 (c)2x2x2x3x3x5

Practice 12

(1)$6\frac{2}{3}$ (2)$\frac{8}{3}$

Practice 13

(1)$\frac{2}{3}$

(2)(a)

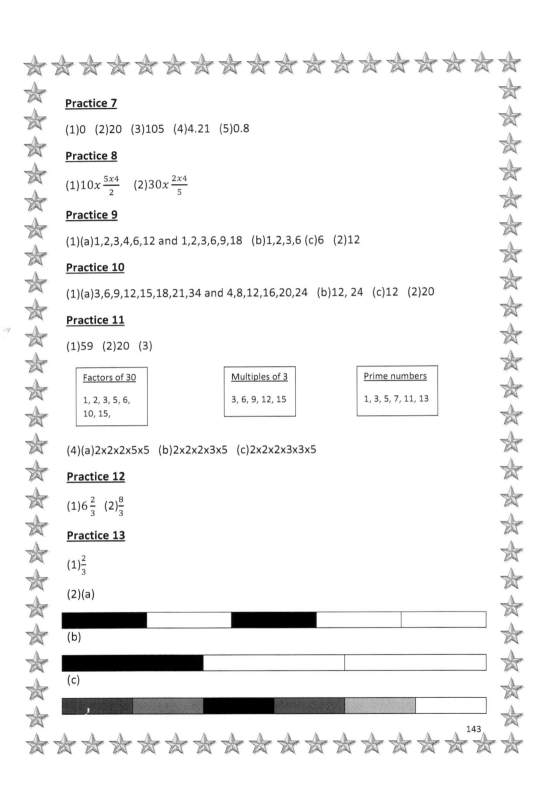

(b)

(c)

143

(3)$\frac{5}{12}$ $[1-(\frac{1}{4}+\frac{1}{3}) = \frac{5}{12}]$

Practice 14

(1)$\frac{1}{7}$, (2)$\frac{1}{9}$, (3)$\frac{1}{7}$, (4)$\frac{2}{3}$, (5)$\frac{3}{4}$

Practice 15

(1)$\frac{8}{10} = \frac{4}{5} = \frac{16}{20}$ (2)$\frac{6}{18}$ (3)$\frac{4}{20}$

Practice 16

(1)$\frac{2}{3}$, (2)$\frac{4}{5}$, (3)$\frac{5}{6}$, (4)$\frac{1}{20}$, (5)$\frac{5}{12}$

Practice 17

(1)$\frac{3}{2}$ (2)$1\frac{5}{12}$ (3)$1\frac{1}{100}$ (4)$3\frac{17}{20}$ (5)8 (6)8 (7)$1\frac{1}{2}$ (8)1 (9)1 (10)$\frac{49}{40}$

Practice 18

1)	02	=	2.0
2)	08.	=	8.0
3)	.50	=	0.5
4)	05	=	005
5)	01	>	0.10
6)	101	>	010
7)	0.20	>	0.02
8)	10	>	01
9)	£0.7	=	£0.70
10)	0.20	<	0.3

Practice 19

(1)0.275   (2)2.65   (3)1.5   (4)0.91   (5)1.2

Practice 20

(1) 0.2000   (2)(a)3.14   (b)3.1

Practice 21

(1)6   (2)1.21   (3)22.6   (4)66.33   (5)240

Practice 22

(1)0.05   (2)0.005   (3)0.15

Practice 23

(1)$\frac{2}{5}$ (2)$\frac{3}{5}$ (3)$\frac{9}{10}$

Practice 24

(1)(a)2.72 (b)2.72 (c)0.272 (d)27.2 (e)0.00272 (2)11.45 (3)9.45 (4)0.925 (5)50.4
(6)19.2 (7)1.32 (8)0.41 (9)13.7 (10)6.16 (11)1.45

Practice 25

(1)10   (2)4   (3)125   (4)2.5litres   (5)(a)£200<£250   (b)£165<£170   (6) 48%

Practice 26

(1)0.2   (2)0.75

Practice 27

(1)£180   (2)£42   (3)£40   (4)1,200,000 or 1.2million (5)

Fraction	Decimal	Percentage
$\frac{1}{5}$	**0.2**	20%
$\frac{17}{20}$	0.85	**85%**
$\frac{1}{100}$	**0.01**	1%

Practice 28

(1)(a)$\frac{PQ}{QR} = 4 \rightarrow PQ = 4QR = 4x100 = 400$. PR = PQ+QR = 400+100=__500m__

(b)$\frac{PQ}{QR} = 4 \rightarrow \frac{20km}{QR} = 4 \rightarrow QR = 5$. PR = PQ + QR = 20km + 5km = __25km__

(c)$\frac{PQ}{QR} = 4 \rightarrow$ PQ = 4QR. PR = PQ + QR = 4QR + QR = 5QR.

So PR = 5QR → 150 = 5QR → QR = <u>30cm</u>

And PQ = 4QR = 4 x 30 =<u>120cm</u>

(2)2cm [$\frac{width}{40m} = \frac{5cm}{100m}$ →width = <u>2cm</u>]

(3)20cm, 9cm [length = $\frac{1}{10}x200cm$ = 20cm], width = $\frac{1}{10}x90cm$ = 9cm]

(4)(a)7.5g [$\frac{200mls \rightarrow 15g}{100mls \rightarrow ?}$ →? = $\frac{15g}{200mls}x100mls$ = <u>7.5g</u>]

(b)75g [$\frac{200mls \rightarrow 15g}{1000mls \rightarrow ?}$ →? = $\frac{15g}{200mls}x1000mls$ = <u>75g</u>]

(c)400mls [$\frac{200mls \rightarrow 15g}{?mls \rightarrow 30g}$ →? = $\frac{200mls}{15g}x30g$ = <u>400mls</u>]

Practice 29

(1)(a)2 (b)6 (c)5   (2)(a)70 (b)70 (c)50   (3)(a)100 (b)400 (c)900   (4)(a)3,000
(b)3,000 (c)5,000   (5)(a)10,000 (b)80,000 (c)70,000   (6)2,000,000 (b)8,000,000
(c)7,000,000   (7)7

(8)

	Round 49,467
To the nearest 10,000	50,000
To the nearest 1,000	49,000
To the nearest 100	49,500

Practice 30

(1)Sign of x is + (positive) and Sign of y is − (negative) (2)(a)A + 3a   (b)T + t + 3q

(c)10m (d)t x t^2

(3)

Tick whether the statement is True or False		
Statement	T	F
A + B = B + A	T	
A − B = B − A		F
A x B = B x A	T	
A ÷ B = B ÷ A		F

(4)(19, 1), (17, 3) (13, 7)

Practice 31

(1)pq+pr   (2)pr+ps+qr+qs   (3)t^2+3t+2   (4)ac-ad+bc-bd   (5)p^2-2p-8

Practice 32

(1)p(q-r)   (2)8n(m-1)   (3)3bc(a+1)

Practice 33

Statement	Expression
I had some money and I gave £20 away	a-£20
I had some money and I gave half of my money away	$a-\dfrac{a}{2}$
I had some money and gave away two third of my money	$a-\dfrac{2a}{3}$
I had some money and I gave 20% of my money away	a-0.2a

Practice 34

(1)156   (2)22   (3)1,000   (4)12   (5)79

Practice 35

(1)(a)C(£) = 8 + 4xR (b)£28   [C = 8 + 4 x 5 = £28] (c)8 [40 = 8 + 4R → R = 8 rides]

(d)10rides, £2 [50 = 8 + 4R → R = 10rides. Then, Cost for 10 rides, C = 8 + 4 x 10 = £48, →change = £50 - £48 = £2].   (2)120. [n x7 + 50 = 890 → n = 120]

Practice 36

(1)1.875m $[\frac{16feet \rightarrow 5metres}{6feet \rightarrow ?}$? $= \frac{5metres \times 6feet}{16feet}$ = 1.875m]

(2)(a)1.8litres $[\frac{150mls \rightarrow 5sec}{?mls \rightarrow 60sec} \rightarrow$? $= \frac{150mls \times 60sec}{5sec}$ = 1800mls = 1.8 litres]

(b)108litres $[\frac{1.8L \rightarrow 1 min}{?L \rightarrow 60min} \rightarrow$? = 1.8 x 60 =108 litres]

Practice 37

(2)(a)Yes. Because the other two angles can be 45°.

each. So 45° + 45° + 90° = 180°.

(b)No. Because 90° + 90° + 90° = 270° which is not Equal to180°.

Practice 38

(1)21ft2, 22ft [A= 3ft x 5ft + 3ft x 2ft = 21ft², P = (6 + 5 + 3 + 3 + 3 + 2)ft = 22ft]

(2)16m x10m – 12m x 6m = 88m² (3) x 60cm → L = 9cm → L² = 81cm²

Practice 39

(a)   150°: 90 + 60

150°

(b)   270°: 90 + 90 + 90

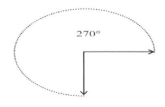

(c)   315°: 90 + 90 + 90 + 45

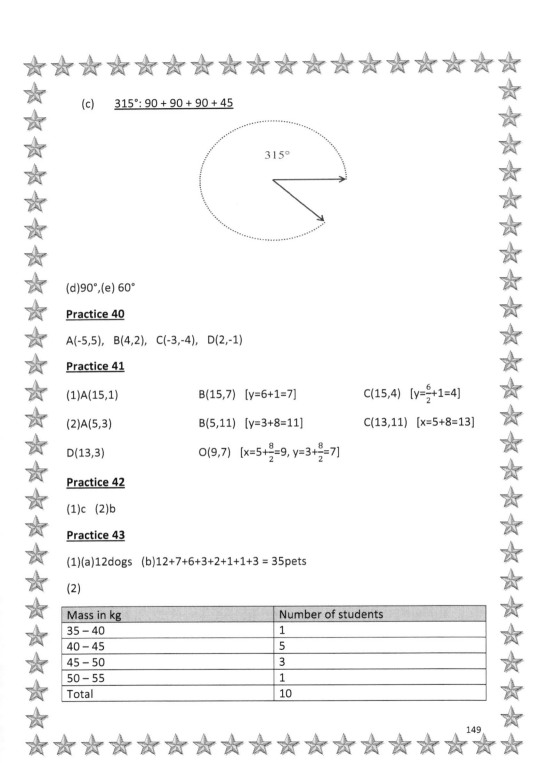

315°

(d)90°,(e) 60°

Practice 40

A(-5,5), B(4,2), C(-3,-4), D(2,-1)

Practice 41

(1)A(15,1)   B(15,7) [y=6+1=7]   C(15,4) [y=$\frac{6}{2}$+1=4]

(2)A(5,3)   B(5,11) [y=3+8=11]   C(13,11) [x=5+8=13]

D(13,3)   O(9,7) [x=5+$\frac{8}{2}$=9, y=3+$\frac{8}{2}$=7]

Practice 42

(1)c   (2)b

Practice 43

(1)(a)12dogs   (b)12+7+6+3+2+1+1+3 = 35pets

(2)

Mass in kg	Number of students
35 – 40	1
40 – 45	5
45 – 50	3
50 – 55	1
Total	10

149

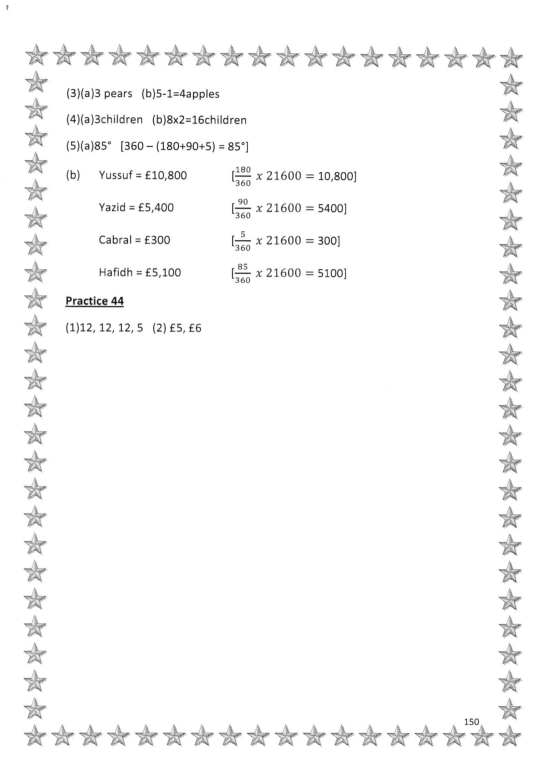

(3)(a)3 pears   (b)5-1=4apples

(4)(a)3children   (b)8x2=16children

(5)(a)85°   [360 − (180+90+5) = 85°]

(b)   Yussuf = £10,800 $[\frac{180}{360} \ x \ 21600 = 10,800]$

Yazid = £5,400 $[\frac{90}{360} \ x \ 21600 = 5400]$

Cabral = £300 $[\frac{5}{360} \ x \ 21600 = 300]$

Hafidh = £5,100 $[\frac{85}{360} \ x \ 21600 = 5100]$

Practice 44

(1)12, 12, 12, 5   (2) £5, £6

ANSWERS TO QUESTION BANK

(1)3495 (2) – 5 (3) 3852 (4)1584 (5)1, 4, <u>10</u>, <u>22</u>, <u>46</u> (6)837 (7)10 (8)20

(9)$2\times3\times5^2$ (10)$\frac{1}{15}$ (11)$\frac{49}{30}$ (12)$\frac{11}{12}$ (13)$\frac{5}{8}$ (14)$2\frac{3}{4}$ (15)$\frac{2}{7}$ (16)$1\frac{1}{50}$ (17)$\frac{15}{18} = \frac{5}{6}$

(18) (a)3.9 $[\frac{325}{100}x\frac{12}{10} = \frac{3900}{1000}]$ (b)13 $[\frac{325}{10}x\frac{12}{30} = \frac{3900}{300}]$(19)480 (20)£45 [50 – 10%of 50]

(21)

Fraction	Decimal	Percentage
$\frac{4}{5}$	0.8	80%
$\frac{13}{25}$	0.52	52%
$\frac{12}{25}$	0.48	48%

(22)14.7m $[\frac{AB}{BC} = 20\rightarrow$ AB = 20BC = 20 x 70cm = 1400cm. AC = AB = BC = 1400 + 70 = 1470cm = 14.7m   (23)2.5m [2.5cm x 100 = 250cm = 2.5m]
(24)(a)24white, (b)16brown   [6w + 4b = 10 $\rightarrow$ 4(6w + 4b) = 10 x 4 $\rightarrow$ 24w + 16b = 40]

(25)

Round to the nearest	5,546,850
Millions	6,000,000
Ten thousands	5,550,000
Thousands	5,547,000
Hundreds	5,546,900

(26)3ab(5ab – 6) (27)$a^2 – b^2$ ..(28)$x^2 – x – 6$ (29)x = 1051 (30)(a)TC(£) = 5+3r+6m (b) £32 [TC= 5 + 3x5 + 6x2 = 32]

(31)(c)$\frac{n}{4} + 10 = 35$ (ii)100 (32)K + M =26 (33) (a)1.8 yards $[\frac{10ft\rightarrow3yd}{6ft\rightarrow?} \rightarrow ? = \frac{6ft\ x\ 3yd}{10ft}$ = 1.8yd] (b)400 feet $[[\frac{10ft\rightarrow3yd}{?\rightarrow120yd} \rightarrow ? = \frac{10ft\ x\ 120yd}{3yd}$ = 400ft]

(34)(b)Time (35)625m^2 [4L = 100m $\rightarrow$ L = 25m, Area = L^2 = (25m)^2 = 625m^2]
(36)140cm^2 [(x+4)+x+(x+4)+x=48 $\rightarrow$ x = 10. Area = (x+4)x = (10=4)x10 = 140cm^2]

(37)30 cm^2 [79 − (7^2) = 30cm^2] (38)50 cm^2 [(14 − 4)(10 − 5) = 50cm^2] (39)4,3
(40) 30 [20+10]

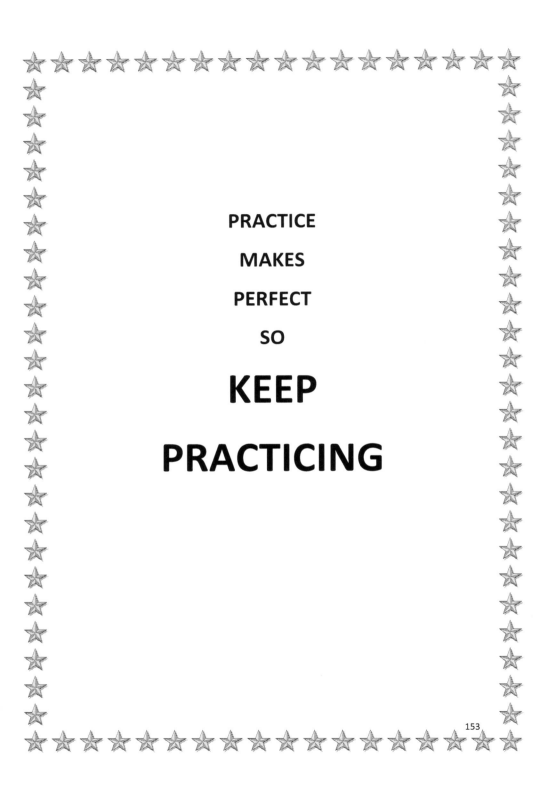

PRACTICE

MAKES

PERFECT

SO

KEEP

PRACTICING

MINI FLASH CARDS

CUT THEM OUT AND KEEP PRACTICING

15 + 17	32 − 19
19 + 16	18 − 15
25 + 14	73 − 25
12 + 29	80 − 17
32 + 45	53 − 12
54 + 37	64 − 25
69 + 96	12 − 7
31 + 89	36 − 28
53 + 72	81 − 53
31 + 69	72 − 41

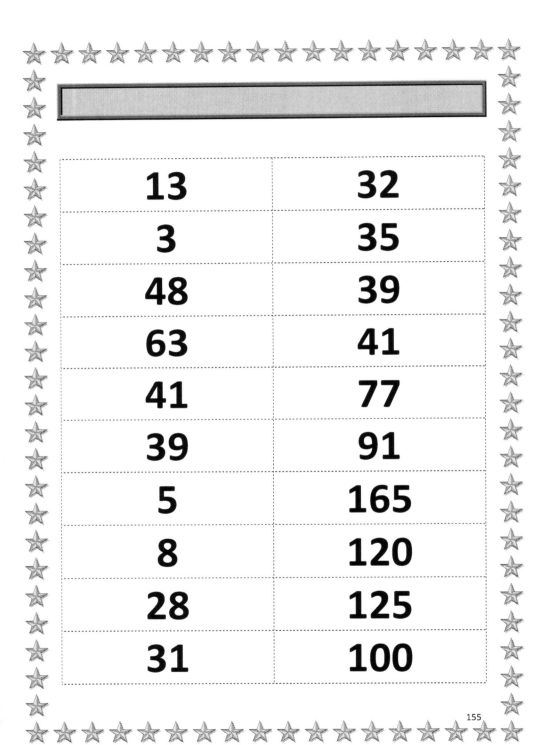

13	32
3	35
48	39
63	41
41	77
39	91
5	165
8	120
28	125
31	100

CUT THEM OUT AND KEEP PRACTICING

12×3	$48 \div 12$
8×5	$72 \div 6$
9×7	$54 \div 9$
12×5	$64 \div 8$
9×8	$45 \div 9$
7×6	$36 \div 6$
4×12	$48 \div 12$
7×8	$42 \div 7$
9×6	$32 \div 8$
6×12	$49 \div 7$

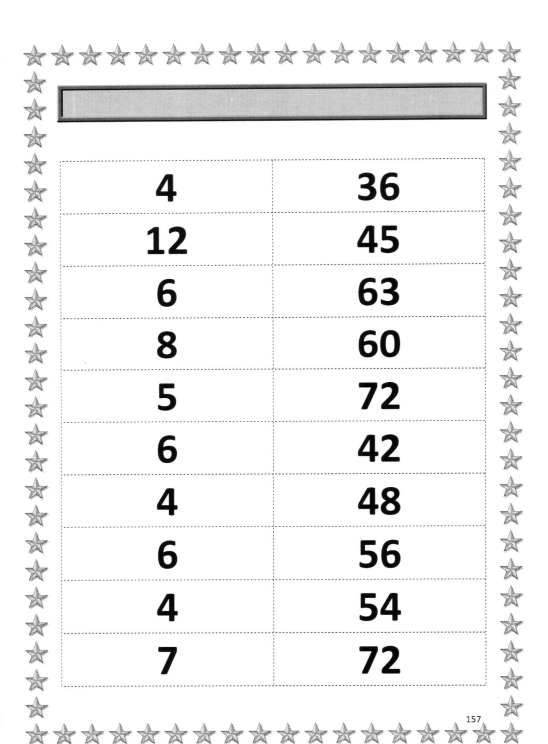

4	36
12	45
6	63
8	60
5	72
6	42
4	48
6	56
4	54
7	72

CONGRATULATION

AIMED TO BUILD STRONG

MATHEMATICAL FOUNDATION

FOR

SECONDARY SCHOOL

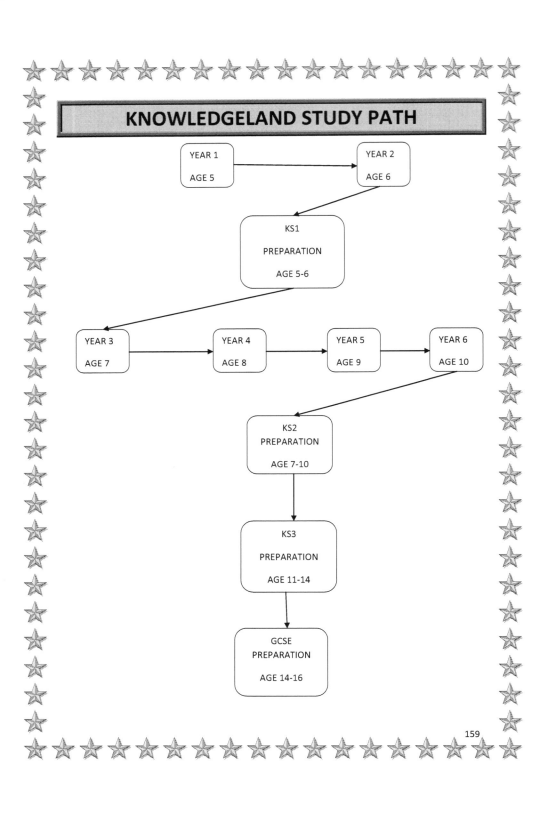

KNOWLEDGELAND STUDY PATH

YEAR 1
AGE 5

YEAR 2
AGE 6

KS1
PREPARATION
AGE 5-6

YEAR 3
AGE 7

YEAR 4
AGE 8

YEAR 5
AGE 9

YEAR 6
AGE 10

KS2
PREPARATION
AGE 7-10

KS3
PREPARATION
AGE 11-14

GCSE
PREPARATION
AGE 14-16

Printed in Poland
by Amazon Fulfillment
Poland Sp. z o.o., Wrocław

62384485R00094